Russell Lewis was born in 1926 and educated at Caerphilly Grammar School and St John's College, Cambridge. From 1966 to 1975 he was Director of the Conservative Political Centre. He is the author of many publications, among them his prophetic *The New Service Society* (1973) and the best-selling *Margaret Thatcher: A Political and Personal Biography*. In 1959 he stood for Parliament as Conservative candidate for Caerphilly, was one of the first Chairmen of the Bow Group and for some years President of the Selsdon Group. He is now a leader-writer on the *Daily Mail*.

Russell Lewis is married with three sons and lives in Surrey.

Also by Russell Lewis

Rome or Brussels
The New Service Society
The Reactionary Joke Book (with Christie Davies)
Margaret Thatcher: A Political and Personal Biography
The Survival of Capitalism
Tony Benn
The Official Shop Steward's Joke Book

ANTI-RACISM
A Mania Exposed

Russell Lewis
With an Introduction by Enoch Powell

Quartet Books
London · New York

First published by Quartet Books Limited 1988
A member of the Namara Group
27/29 Goodge Street
London W1P 1FD

British Library Cataloguing in Publication Data

Lewis, Russell
    Anti-racism: a mania exposed.
    1. Great Britain – Race relations
    I. Title
    305.8′ 00941   DA125.A1

ISBN 0 7043 0070 2

Typeset by MC Typeset Limited, Chatham, Kent

Reproduced, printed and bound in Great Britain by
Hazell Watson & Viney Limited
Member of BPCC plc
Aylesbury Bucks

To Robert Conquest,
veteran exposer of
tyranny and cant

CONTENTS

ACKNOWLEDGEMENTS

I should like to express my gratitude to the following for advice, material and ideas for this book: Christie Davies, Professor of Sociology, Reading University; Lord Bauer, Professor of Economics at the London School of Economics; Digby Anderson, Director of the Social Affairs Unit; George Gardner, MP; Christine Chapman of BBC Television; Peter Burden, Crime Correspondent of the *Daily Mail*; Anthony Doran, Local Government Correspondent of the *Daily Mail*. I would also like to thank: Derek Hill, chief leader-writer of the *Daily Express*; Ronald Spark, chief leader-writer of the *Sun*; Stuart Butler, Director of Domestic Policy Studies at the Heritage Foundation, Washington, and my ever-helpful colleagues in the *Daily Mail* library.

RUSSELL LEWIS

INTRODUCTION

by Enoch Powell

After the Second World War the British were the victims of an event for which nothing in their history or experience had prepared them. Britain – the United Kingdom, that is – had been unlike all other countries in the world in not having its own citizenship. Its belongers, to use a convenient paraphrase for citizen, were subjects, persons born or naturalized within the allegiance. The only status which the people of the United Kingdom possessed therefore expanded so that it comprised all the hundreds of millions of inhabitants of the Empire and Commonwealth under the rule of the Crown. Every one of those individuals thereby had citizen's right in the United Kingdom: the right to enter, work and live in the country.

Until the late 1940s few of the inhabitants of the Empire had been in a position to avail themselves of that right; but, with cheap transport and an inflation-fed demand for labour in Britain, a flood of immigrants began in the late 1940s, initially, in the main, from the West Indies, but thereafter from Asia and Africa.

The Labour government of the day was appalled at the foreseeable consequences and cast about for means to prevent the inflow. To do so, however, it would be necessary to limit citizen right in the United Kingdom to those born there or closely connected with it by birth. A bill to make this change in the law, which was not expected to be unduly controversial, had been prepared before Winston Churchill's resignation in 1955. Had it been passed at that time, the change in the United Kingdom's population would have remained negligible. In fact, the legislation was delayed until 1961 and did not come into force until July 1962,* by which time 'race' had become a politically emotive subject in white countries and a further influx into the United Kingdom had taken place of such dimensions that even in the terms of the 1962 legislation it would be self-perpetuating.

This was not understood at the time. It was still possible after 1962 to write, as I did in February1967: 'The best I dare to hope is that by the end of the century we shall be left not with a growing and more menacing phenomenon but with fixed and almost traditional "foreign" areas in certain towns and cities.' I added that 'even this relatively happy outcome implies that vigorous action to limit and if possible reduce total numbers is taken as from now'. In fact, since 1965 assisted voluntary repatriation had been part of the official policy of the Conservative opposition; but during the late 1960s the scale of what had happened was revealed by statistics (official from 1969 onwards) of the proportion of total births, locality by locality, where the parents were born in the New Commonwealth. These gave a reliable indication of the composition of the future population and made it clear that 'by the end of the century' the phenomenon would indeed be 'growing and more menacing', without taking account of any subsequent nett immigration.

The response of political parties and governments to the facts, which they now understood, was twofold. One reaction was to dismiss the figures and their implications. The other was to attempt to avert the consequences by regulating the lawful relations between one individual or group in the population and another. In 1965 'race' was for the first time introduced into the law of the United Kingdom as a ground on which one citizen would be treated differently from another.

That tentative beginning was followed in 1968 by the introduction of civil and criminal sanctions to be administered by a body specially created for the purpose; and the scope of the legislation was widened and the functions of the invigilating commission were

---

* A flaw in drafting, not corrected until 1968, unintentionally left citizen right still vested in those inhabitants of Commonwealth countries who did not become citizens of those countries upon the attainment of independence.

extended in 1976. The havoc wrought by this fundamental change in our law is the theme of Mr Russell Lewis's book. He unfolds the unhappy story, step by step; and few readers will remain unpersuaded that the legislative and administrative innovation has been self-defeating, if its real intention was to allay anxieties and animosities and to reduce the scope for mutual hostility between different sections of the population. Britain, as he shows, is now headed for the imposition of quotas in terms of colour upon private undertakings and upon government and Crown services; nor will the armed forces long remain immune.

Mr Lewis's remedy is simple and radical: eliminate racial discrimination from the statute book, and let all be once more indistinguishable in the eyes of the law. Consistently with the general philosophy of the present government, competitive disadvantages under which newcomers labour will be soonest removed if the enterprise and initiative of the individual or the group is allowed free play. Mr Lewis is too sincere to conceal his disbelief that there will in fact be any such change of policy. A Prime Minister who was sharply warned off the course when in 1978 she stumbled into a casual reference to the prevalent public fear of being 'swamped', has been as resolute as Edward Heath not to allow that particular reform on to her agenda. That being so, the imagination is overtaxed to envisage a government or a parliamentary majority which will dare to send the Commission for Racial Equality packing and repeal the Race Relations Acts of 1968 and 1976.

That is not the only reason why I cannot share the author's optimistic belief that, while 'anti-racism, the quango kingdom which we have produced to counter what is a very real social problem', is to be deplored, the problem itself 'should gradually fade through normal human contact'. Would that were so! The age-structure of the present New Commonwealth ethnic population ensures that in the foreseeable future it will constitute one third or more of the population of Inner London and of cities and areas up and down England. That will be more than sufficient in our elective democracy to secure for it effective political control locally and nationally by dint of its distinctiveness and its solidarity. I have never been able to convince myself that this point could be reached or approached without civil strife of a degree that makes it indistinguishable from civil war. That outcome will be hastened, but it will not have been caused, by the anti-racist mania which is the subject of this book.

J. ENOCH POWELL,
London SW1, January 1988

ANTI-RACISM, A MANIA EXPOSED

1

A Mania for Our Time

Every age has its 'isms' and in ours 'racism' has come to the fore. It is an ugly word for what those most given to using it claim to be an ugly feature of Britain today, namely, an unreasoning dislike among the majority white population of ethnic minority groups, especially those with dark skins. That is what it means when used in good faith. Unhappily it is often used not to analyse but to bully, not as an ordinary adjective but as a term of abuse. The point has been well put by Ray Honeyford, former headmaster of Drummond Middle School, Bradford:

A 'racist' is to the race relations lobby what 'Protestant' was to the inquisitors of the Counter-Reformation, or witches to the seventeenth-century burghers of Salem. It is the totem of the new doctrine of anti-racism. Its definition varies according to the purpose it is meant to achieve. It is a gift to the zealot, since he can apply it to anyone who disagrees with him – and he often ejaculates the word as though it were a synonym for 'rapist' or 'fascist'. It takes its force not from its power to describe but from its power to coerce and intimidate. It is attached to anyone who challenges the arguments or rhetoric of the race relations lobby. It is more a weapon than a word.[1]

Racism is a serious social disease but the recommended cure, anti-racism, can be as fatal. Of course no decent person disputes that racial hatred and strife are deplorable and no one who has any memory or knowledge of the Nazi era can doubt that they have

1

been among the most awful curses ever to afflict mankind. Yet, in this country at least, there is as much reason to worry about the antics of many of those who proclaim themselves 'anti-racists' as about the 'racism' they claim to see all around them. A favourite accusation of those who campaign against racial prejudice in Britain is that this country is one in which racism is firmly institutionalized, indeed endemic in the whole way of life of the majority of its citizens. Yet as much to be deplored is institutionalized anti-racism, the quango kingdom which we have produced to counter what is a very real social problem, but one which through normal human contact should gradually fade.

By 'anti-racism' I mean the doctrine of resistance to the supposed prejudice of the white majority in Britain against its non-white fellow-citizens. This prejudice, it is alleged, produces such oppressive discrimination that violent racial conflict is inevitable unless we as a society accept an interventionist political and administrative regime fundamentally hostile to our traditional free institutions.

A striking statement of this view, remarkable not so much for its extremism, though that is execrable enough, but for its appalling frankness, has been made by Professor Chris Mullard:

> The battle will be a bloody one. Black and white will have no choice. The liberals . . . will be caught in the middle. In the end they too will have no choice – they will have to side with black or white . . .
> Blacks will fight with pressure, leaflets, campaigns, demonstrations, fists and scorching resentment, which, when peaceful means fail, will explode into street-fighting, urban guerilla warfare, looting, burning and rioting. Critics will argue smugly that this cannot possibly happen here. Most of them will be white, blind to what is already happening, wrapped in cocoons of isolation and utopian dreams of multi-racialism, confident that white is might.
> To these I say 'Watch out Whitey, nigger goin' to get you!'[2]

The British educationist who wrote these words cannot be dismissed as an unrepresentative rabble-rouser. On the contrary he is a leading light in the 'anti-racist' movement in Britain. He has been Director of the Race Relations Policy and Practice Unit at the London University of Education, Britain's largest teacher-training college, and is now Professor of Race and Ethnic Relations at the University of Amsterdam.

One object of this book is to expose and to rebut this altogether too prevalent libel of a people unusual if anything for their tolerance and celebrated for their tradition of justice and fair play. Even in the heyday of racialist theories among intellectuals a century ago the British paid hardly any attention to such bogus biology. In Britain no racialist party has ever caught on. In parliamentary elections Fascist and other extreme nationalist parties have never collected more than derisory numbers of votes. All the major parties have shunned racist extremism. There has always been a good deal of *patriotism*, that is love of one's country, among the British, and there still is, though it tends to come to the surface only in times of national danger and surprises even themselves by its intensity, as for instance during the Falklands campaign. Yet in spite of having had for a time an enormous empire, they have precious little missionary urge to impose on others the British way of life.

At its best, British colonialism was distinguished by a policy of indirect rule and live-and-let-live, as far as possible leaving its subjects to abide by their own customs. The exclusiveness of the British colonists' clubs was the reverse side of this coin. And arguably, such exclusiveness was more snobbish than racist: the British middle and upper classes, especially in the Edwardian period, which was also the high noon of empire, were just as exclusive towards the working class at home.

For the sole example of the expulsion from Britain of a group of people on account of their race one must go back to the thirteenth century when Edward I expelled the Jews. They were readmitted under Cromwell and by the nineteenth century one of their number, Disraeli, had become Prime Minister, and a Tory one at that. During most of their history the British have provided a refuge for those of all races who fled from persecution overseas, including Karl Marx and the proponents of international communism who came to study revolution in the reading room of the British Museum under Marx's watchful eye.

Of course, no one who knows anything about Anglo-Irish history will say that Britain has an untarnished record for racial harmony. But the national flag, the Union Jack, does symbolize

3

the unity in diversity of the English, Welsh, Scots and Irish. Their population movements were certainly not accomplished without conflicts, but in time these have been largely resolved with minimal legislative intervention. Those who moved from one corner of these islands to another made their own arrangements through the free market about food, shelter, leisure and work. And, on the whole, they were gradually assimilated into the surrounding population. By contrast the settlement of the 2.5 million or so immigrants from the New Commonwealth and Pakistan in the interventionist era since the end of the Second World War has created an important new area of state activity and inevitably pushed it into the political domain. A significant fact about Professor Mullard is that so much of his work has been funded by the public purse.

Of course there are many others, mostly less prominent than he and far less objectionable, who are also concerned with race relations and likewise dependent, directly or indirectly, on the taxpayer. These have been collectively dubbed the 'race relations industry', which, not surprisingly, is resented as a cheap gibe by those who belong to or are associated with it. So let it be clear that the object of this work is not to ridicule the efforts of those who sincerely seek better relations between the races but to examine critically and question the highly politicized methods of pursuing that worthy objective in Britain today.

What is or who are the race relations industry? Tom Hastie provides a striking definition:

> By 'race industry' I mean community relations personnel, multi-ethnic education inspectors and advisers, vote-hungry local politicians, members of local government committees and agencies set up for example to monitor police attitudes to blacks, ambitious leaders of immigrant pressure groups and the like. In other words, those with a vested interest in putting race into the forefront of people's minds.[3]

He adds that the result is 'Newsam's Law',[4] which runs, 'The incidence of alleged racism in a given society will vary in a direct proportion to the number of people handsomely paid to find it.' Or, as the old saying bluntly puts it, 'Never ask the barber if you need a haircut.'

It may be objected that this is a case of generalizing on the basis of a few particulars, yet, judging by some of the absurdities which anti-racist extremists have imposed in recent times on the council staff and citizens of boroughs where they have assumed control, Tom Hastie's definition is a fair one. The councils concerned are those with substantial (15% or more) ethnic minorities, and it must be said that, on the whole, the larger the ratio of sectional interests the more radical the council's behaviour becomes. This suggests that they are not so much 'loony left' as is often suggested, but motivated by a perfectly rational desire to win votes. Appeals to a variety of sectional interests – blacks, Asians, gays and Irish supporters of Sinn Fein – are a fairly new phenomenon in part pioneered by Ken Livingstone, leader in the last years of the Greater London Council. He was quite open about his intention of using ratepayers' money to subsidize a constituency of activist minority supporters which added together, especially in local elections where there is normally a very small percentage turnout, could make all the difference between victory and defeat.

Ken Livingstone's new parliamentary constituency, Brent, is a good place to begin a brief tour of the follies perpetrated by left-wing town councils in the name of anti-racism. There are strong indications that Brent council is attempting to drive out white headteachers by a campaign of intimidation. The most notorious case has been that of infants' school headmistress Mrs Maureen McGoldrick, who was accused by a junior official on the council's education committee of making a racist remark. She denied having made the remark and was unanimously cleared of doing so by the school governors. The council none the less persisted in suspending her and trying to make her appear before a disciplinary hearing. She was freed from this persecution only after court cases which went as far as Appeal and the intervention of the Education Secretary of State.[5]

In 1986 at Willesden High School, also in Brent, a school governor of aggressive appearance, called Kuba Assegai, intimidated many of the teachers by interrupting their lessons. He told the children there that the Americans had developed a bomb to kill only black people. Teachers were afraid to complain in case they were branded 'racist'.

Another bizarre tale from Brent was of a school governor, Mrs

Maureen Geldman, who for looking at her watch – she was apparently already late for an appointment – while a black teacher was being interviewed for a headship, was accused of 'racist body language' and dropped from the interview panel.[6]

It was perhaps not surprising after all this to learn that Brent council had contributed £5,000 a year to a project in which anti-racist officers led by Professor Mullard, mentioned above, toured schools looking for examples of colour prejudice.[7] This however was a modest enterprise compared with a much more ambitious scheme, confined to the borough, to appoint over 180 race watchdogs in the schools. Their job was to report on teaching and even check on school textbooks to make sure they gave the right image of black people. Up to £5 million of the taxpayers' money was to be used for this exercise.[8]

Turning now to Islington, a clerk in the housing department was suspended in April 1984 for failing to ask a black colleague to the office Christmas lunch. The left-wing council leaders decided that she was guilty of race harassment, gave her a written warning and a reprimand and ordered her to go on a racist-awareness course. After attending her course the clerk expected to go back to work but she was still suspended the following February, because the activists of the NALGO union refused to work with her.[9]

The complaint against the clerk, Mrs Pledger, had been lodged by her colleague, Miss Linda Braithwaite, who had not been asked to the Christmas lunch. She later complained that Miss Vi Howell, to whom she was an assistant, had ticked her off in front of other staff. Miss Howell was reprimanded for racial harassment. This did not however satisfy members of NALGO who demanded that she sign a written confession branding her action 'wrong and discriminatory'. When she refused the union called its 600 members out on strike but only half of them complied and Miss Howell returned to work.[10] Mrs Pledger's situation, however, was as unresolved as ever. It was only after another year, by which time she had been suspended on full pay for eighteen months, that she was given £10,000 to go quietly.[11]

Around the time that the strike was fizzling out, Islington council was advertising for an £11,000-a-year 'adviser on anti-racist strategies' in primary schools.[12] It also announced that a waiting-list for homes owned by the borough was to be restricted to black applicants.[13] More recently the council made a grant of

6

£750 for the recording and distribution of anti-racist songs.[14]

Some of the teachers in Islington appear to be afflicted with the same obsession. English staff at Islington's Holloway School condemned Roald Dahl's children's classic *Charlie and the Chocolate Factory*, which has sold two million copies in Britain alone, as 'rotten to the core' and banned it from the classrooms. This initiative was welcomed by the Inner London Education Authority (which, incidentally, is one of the highest spenders and has among the worst results of all the regional educational authorities in the kingdom). ILEA voted 'not to recommend its use' in its other schools when teachers enquired after the book.[15]

In the London borough of Lewisham the council voted to delete the word 'black' from all its publications in order not to offend coloured people. Terms such as 'accident black spot' were prohibited and trade unionists would find themselves 'boycotting' a job instead of 'blacking' it. A public relations person explaining the move told a reporter, 'For the same reason we will not use the word blackmail – although the occasion hasn't arisen and I don't quite know what we would use instead.'[16]

Lewisham council also recently scrapped an arts festival which had been going for twenty-seven years because it was too competitive and did not involve enough black people. Instead the events would be spread out over the year and the musical talent competitions, for which there would be no first, second or third places and no prizes, would emphasize ethnic minority music instead of the classics.

Hackney is London's poorest borough. In 1985, the ruling Labour group set a target for one in three of the town hall staff to be coloured.[17] When a white, Anthony Hughes, applied for a post as a trainee gardener with Hackney council he was turned down, because the department was only taking on blacks. He took the council to an industrial tribunal where it was found guilty of racial discrimination and had to pay £350 in compensation.[18] Similarly a council scheme for holidays for pensioners from the borough's Asian, African, Caribbean, Cypriot and orthodox Jewish communities, was condemned by the Commission for Racial Equality as racially discriminatory.[19] But what looked like an attempt at reverse discrimination went further than that. Hackney was the first local authority in the country to put into effect the policy of asking everybody applying to it, not only for jobs but for planning permission or a home help, to fill in a form stating their racial origin. With regard to this the Commission for Racial Equality dismissed fears that such information could be used to promote discrimination but added that the council should make it clear that to answer the question was not compulsory. Yet if the answers given were not to be used in order to promote discrimination it is difficult to see what possible use they could be. This is a dilemma of so-called 'racial monitoring' to which I shall return later.

Another scheme of Hackney council which reflected the same philosophy and immediately ran into trouble was to change the current English names of the streets into ethnic ones, so that Britannia Walk, for example, would become Shaheed-e-Azam Bhagot-Singh Avenue. Bhagot Singh was an Indian 'freedom fighter', who resented the British and was sentenced to death in the 1930s for terrorism. Not surprisingly a residents' group was formed to resist the proposal, maintaining that the scheme was itself racist and calculated to create antagonism against other races among white residents, though they had always lived in harmony before.[20]

That some people in Hackney were not devoted to the cause of racial harmony was indicated in January 1986 when the Hackney Black People's Association invited controversial Black Muslim Louis Farrakhan to be their guest. This angered Hackney's Jewish community, for Farrakhan was on record as describing Judaism as a 'gutter religion' and Hitler as a 'great man'. The association's Lester Lewis, a Labour councillor who had extended the invitation, was unrepentant, refusing to accept that Farrakhan was an anti-Semite and asserting that the quotes were taken out of context. In the event the Home Secretary refused to allow Farrakhan to enter the country, though that did not diminish the row.[21]

In 1986 the neighbouring borough of Haringey also made its bid for inclusion in the increasingly bizarre history of anti-racist council policy with the sacking of a wages clerk from its community affairs department for racial harassment. The clerk, Mrs Shirley Scott, was dismissed for placing on her office desk a banana-shaped pen which she had earlier used as a prop at a fancy dress concert. It was said to have given offence to a colleague, Miss Desai, but Mrs Scott said, 'It's crazy. We never had a cross word.'[22]

Another victim of the inquisitorial policy now prevalent in many left-wing inner London boroughs was Jack Fuller, principal of Waltham Forest College, who had the temerity to write to *The Times* and say that West Indian intruders were responsible for a great deal of robbery and vandalism on the campus.[23] Inevitably he was called before the board of governors to answer a charge of 'racism', a particularly inappropriate accusation since he was married to a Malaysian Chinese.

The London borough of Lambeth, once considered the capital of Cockney culture – it was after all the birthplace of the Lambeth Walk – has now, under the council leadership of the strident Ms Linda Bellos, become almost the Mecca of extremism. Its approach to racial matters was indicated in its order to a fifteen-year-old teenage girl to attend special therapy sessions with a black psychologist. This was because the girl had expressed a wish to live with white foster parents. That, according to the council, suggested she was mentally disturbed.

Unfortunately this kind of misdirected and so often counter-productive zeal is not restricted to the capital. Look westward to Bristol, which before the industrial revolution was England's second city and grew rich on the trade in sugar, tea, tobacco and cotton. Far from welcoming the idea put forward by National Heritage for setting up a 'museum of empire' in the summer of 1986, Bristol's left-wing rulers thought it would be 'inflammatory and disrespectful' to ethnic minorities from former British colonies living there.[24] That same year, Jon Savery was brought before a disciplinary tribunal to answer claims that he was racist. In particular he was arraigned for writing an article in the obscure but intellectually high-quality right-wing journal, the *Salisbury Review*. In it he alleged that the virulent brand of anti-racism practised by those who encouraged their children to taunt the likes of Ray Honeyford was akin not to a belief in equality but to a witch-hunt. Mr Savery's main offence, however, was that he had opposed a move by the local race lobby to scrap Scale Four teaching posts at the Bristol Multi-Cultural Education Centre and advertise them exclusively for black applicants. He had the temerity to suggest that this idea, which came from a small group of teachers known as MACAW (Multi-Cultural Afro-Caribbean-Asian Working Group), was unfair. Like many of the people who have been accused of being racist (for instance Mrs McGoldrick, the target of self-styled anti-racists in the London borough of Brent, who was immensely popular with ethnic staff and parents), Jon Savery was quite the reverse. He married a West Indian when he was twenty-seven and, though subsequently divorced, had remained on friendly terms with his wife's family. In the event he was cleared of the charge but told to leave his school the day after he shared a platform with Ray Honeyford at a Bristol University Conservative Students' Association meeting on free speech in October 1986. Members of the National Union of Teachers demonstrated outside the meeting in an attempt to prevent him from speaking. He also had trouble at his workplace where forty teachers at the Multi-Cultural Centre who were 'committed to anti-racism' had refused to work with him.[25]

Let us move next to the West Midlands, to Wolverhampton, where Enoch Powell, for long the race lobby's most implacable foe, was once MP. He has long departed but the follies he denounced live on. The most notable of these recently was the attempt of Labour councillor Phil Richards to have Elgar's 'Land of Hope and Glory' banned from a Festival of Remembrance. He said, 'I would not wish to have this racist song repeated in our multi-cultural community.' He added, 'To older members of ethnic groups whose viewpoint of empire is different from our own it is downright offensive. I would rather it was replaced by "Jerusalem" or the "Battle Hymn of the Republic".'[26]

Leeds is, many would say, a city which epitomizes the Yorkshire no-nonsense attitude to life, yet it recently contributed its own bit of nonsense to the literature of 'anti-racism'. It was reported in December 1986 that Mrs Gillian Robb-Webb, head teacher at the multi-racial Chapel Allerton Primary School, Leeds, had rewritten the story of *Goldilocks and the Three Bears*. She was concerned that the heroine's golden curls might alienate black children listening to the story. 'We are very mindful of the racial sensitivity in the school,' she told a reporter. 'Most important to us is a child's self-esteem. The blonde idea of a pretty little girl in the Goldilocks story ought to be changed. Apart from that, as a feminist I don't like the idea of the pretty little girl who, if you reason it out, turns to crime'; a fine example, incidentally, of how one absurdity can reinforce another. In any event Goldilocks became Jackie. The bears, inexplicably, became frogs and the old fairy tale re-emerged as *Jackie and the Three Frogs*. It was also reported that children in the reception class were learning to recite an updated nursery rhyme, 'Baa Baa White Sheep'.[27]

As a case of misguided interference with fairy-tale symbols, this is reminiscent of the row in Liverpool about golliwogs. Toxteth, a district in Liverpool with a substantial black population, was the scene of serious riots in 1981. One imaginative attempt to repair damage caused by the riots was the launching of Liverpool's £30 million International Garden Festival, which was opened by the Queen in May 1984. One of its prime features was a fairy-tale Jam Garden for children, provided by Robertson's Jam. In the garden were nine giant jars of Robertson's jam, on each of which was Robertson's trademark, Mr Golly. This Mr Keva Coombes, Labour leader of Merseyside County Council, condemned as insulting to the Toxteth area's multi-racial community. He demanded that the jars be withdrawn. But after a long talk with Merseyside Development Corporation, which was staging the festival, he unexpectedly beat a retreat: it turned out that the Jam Garden had been designed and built by Mr Coombes' own council.[28]

Of course, golliwogs have always been anathema to the race relations lobby. It alleged that the dolls are demeaning stereotypes which black people find offensive, but there is plenty of evidence to contradict this view. Charlie Williams, for instance, the popular black northern comic, said, 'The golliwog has been around for as long as I can remember. To me it's just a friendly toy for kids. If I wanted to make a joke I'd say, "Me? Bitter and resentful? Never. I thought it was a good photograph!"' Regarding the campaign against Robertson's Golly he said, 'When I read about it, it struck me as quite funny. But when I got to thinking I realized it was really just sad. The more I think about it the more I believe a campaign like this is going to do more harm than good to the cause of race relations.' Nor does Robertson's symbol appear to upset any of the blacks among the 840 workers in its factory. One coloured worker at the Robertson's Golden Shred works was reported as saying, 'I bought a golliwog for my two children. Peter loved him when he was a baby and now Jessica takes the doll to bed every night. I don't think that there is any racial significance in the golliwog at all. It has never occurred to me to be offended.'[29]

The original golliwog was a soft toy made from mothers' threadbare black skirts with scraps of white blouse for eyes, mouth

11

and shirt. It was called 'Golly' by toddlers who couldn't quite manage 'dolly'. It was discovered by one of the Robertson family while travelling around rural America at the turn of the century. He found it so appealing that he adopted it as the firm's official trademark and mascot and launched it as a badge in 1930, since when over twenty million have been issued. It has been a constant target of the race relations bodies but they have been largely unable to undermine the affection with which the dolls are regarded by most people, including blacks. All the same, the pressure groups have had some success. In 1971 Raleigh changed the name of a new trike from Gay Golly (an admittedly unhappy combination) to Baby Bunny. In 1975, when *Noddy* appeared on television the three naughty golliwogs were replaced by Frenchmen. In August 1985, after protests from a race relations worker from Hackney, Liberty's withdrew Golliwog teapots, egg cups and mugs.[30] In January 1987 a new edition of Enid Blyton's works appeared with the golliwogs written out altogether and replaced by naughty gnomes. The explanation of the publishers, Macdonald's, that this change had nothing to do with pressure from anti-racists but was instituted because today's children do not know what golliwogs are, seemed a little lame.[31]

What these examples, which could be multiplied, show is how widespread the anti-racism mania has become in Britain. To dub it a mania is not unfair. The tone of those in the grip of it is akin to that of the hell-fire preacher: self-righteous and intolerant. Many of them intimidate more than they persuade, and how could it be otherwise? How could anyone expect a teacher to react to a 'race-awareness course' with anything but anger at such an insult to his or her intelligence? What kind of mentality is abroad that could bring even the most militant trade unionists to demand that a woman council employee in Islington should make a public confession of racism or lose her job because the other union members would otherwise refuse to work with her?

At its most extreme this attitude is reminiscent of the witch-hunt and it is by no means new. Witches are thought of as rather a joke nowadays and few realize what a dreadful chapter in sixteenth- and seventeenth-century European history the hunting of witches actually was. Under intolerable pressure, such as the rack and the thumbscrew, thousands of people, most of them old women, were induced to confess to unspeakable crimes. We are of course a long way from reintroducing such persecution in Britain, but the urge to coerce people into verbally subscribing to beliefs which they do not accept of their own free will – as when teachers applying for a job in certain boroughs run by left-wing councils are obliged to utter ritual condemnations of racism as a condition of employment – is alive and far too well.

Many of the key figures in the race relations industry are politically motivated, but others have a purely professional interest in magnifying the importance of the task which, after all, keeps them gainfully employed. That would not matter so much were it not for the mounting threat which such people pose to the freedom of ordinary citizens to work or enjoy themselves without gratuitous and arbitrary interference.

It is no good adopting an attitude of 'let sleeping dogs lie' and assuming that, given time, the problem will simply recede. The race relations industry has a momentum of its own. Those within it who do genuinely believe in the gospel they preach have every incentive to show proof that race relations are getting worse, for that makes their message all the more urgent. Others are not concerned with highlighting racial problems in order that they may be more quickly solved, but are actually in the business of promoting social strife. Instead of integrating the different races into our community these people are seeking to set them against each other. They don't want the foundations of society strengthened but to have them undermined. Their aim is revolutionary and they are thus intent on creating a constituency of malcontents in preparation for the grand assault on our social order which they believe is only a matter of time. This book aims to make their task more difficult and to bring some corrective reasoning into an area where irrational sloganizing has become endemic. In particular I shall try to:

Present the facts which I believe repudiate the charge so often levelled by the race relations lobby that Britain is a profoundly racist society.

Indicate the influence of the race relations industry in Britain, both in its scale and effect.

Show that all too often the activities of the race relations lobby do not advance the interests of the ethnic minorities they are meant to serve, but weaken instead of strengthening their economic position and can even foster popular resentment against the ethnics instead of enlisting goodwill.

Highlight the positive side to the picture, especially the ethnic minorities' successful responses to the demands and pressures of life in Britain.

Argue that the way forward for the immigrant groups is to concentrate on improving their own and their families' material conditions rather than seeking through political activism compensatory privileges and rights.

Suggest an institutional framework for better race relations, including the shrinkage of the Commission for Racial Equality and other lesser bodies and the opening-up of the free market, the great virtue of which is that it is colour-blind.

2

The Emotional Fuels of Anti-Racism

Of all the great issues which perplex and divide our society, nuclear weapons, civil liberties and so on, none, I believe, is more dangerous than racism. What makes racism unlike all other political problems is that it is the product of the irrational and is therefore not easily dealt with by ordinary discourse. We are all victims of the poison of racial prejudice. Racism is part of the fabric of our history, woven into our imperial past and although we have shed our colonies – or most of them – we have not succeeded in shedding the ideologies and attitudes which underpinned our economic and military subjugation of other races and cultures . . . We have to recognize – whether we like it or not – that Britain is a multi-racial society.

The above comment is by Jacob Ecclestone, Deputy General Secretary of the National Union of Journalists, in the foreword of a book produced by the Campaign Against Racism in the Media, with the unlikely and unlovely title *It ain't Half Racist, Mum.*[1] It is characteristic of the approach of many of the anti-racist lobby. It is exaggeratedly alarmist (is racism really the most dangerous issue of our time?). It affects the voice of sweet reason, and by implication contrasts it with the dark irrational urges which are supposed to direct the thoughts and actions of all who disagree with its sentiments. It justifies these sentiments by an appeal to history which is one-sided and little less than a libel on our nation's past. And it ends with an implied threat that, if we know what's good for us, we had better accept the blindingly obvious – that

15

Britain is now a multi-racial society. What, one wonders, does Mr Ecclestone think we were before? To suggest that British multi-racialism is a new phenomenon is, for instance, insulting to the Welsh, an ethnic minority to which this author belongs. It is equally a slight upon the Scots, Irish, Jews, Poles, Ukrainians and numerous others. The whole point about Britain's evolution is that we are publicly and politically one nation but privately a mosaic of coexisting peoples. A British Sikh, Hindu, Muslim, Bengali, Tamil or Barbadian is as welcome as a British Jew, Pole or Irishman. All who accept our public traditions are guaranteed the safety of their private traditions in their own homes, because their home is their castle.

There is no worse advice one can give to any immigrant group in any country than to attack that country's traditions and identity. If I were to emigrate to Australia I would not be a 'wingeing Pom' but a 'fair dinkum Aussie Pom'. If I took off to America I wouldn't expect my offspring to be taught to honour George III. If I went to India, I would treat every sacred cow with proper respect. Most immigrants understand this, especially those who are businessmen and need to cultivate customers – like the Muslim grocer who runs an off-licence. Yet such commonsense is apparently resented by many race relations professionals who feel compelled endlessly to emphasize the separateness of people.

The basic objection to the sort of view propagated by Mr Ecclestone and others is a comparative one. It is in fact easier to be a member of even a visible ethnic minority in Britain than in most countries in the world. I would rather be a Tamil in the United Kingdom than in Sri Lanka, a Sikh in Southall than in New Delhi, a black man in Cardiff than in Kosice, Czechoslovakia (where the gypsies are black in the white Slovak population), or in North India, a Chinese in London than in Malaysia. It is far pleasanter to be an African student in any British university than at Patrice Lumumba University in Moscow, the establishment set aside for the education of students from the Third World and especially Africa, which is really a means of segregating them from the Russians – a Soviet version of apartheid.

Nor should Britain feel any need to apologize for its strong sense of identity, which is neither racist nor ideological. In many countries of the Third World there is much talk about 'nation-building', that is to say the creation of the sort of national unity we

16

have constructed over the centuries. Why then should we be expected to dismantle or deny *our* nationhood? In a world of nation states, if nationality depends on ideology (as in the Soviet Union) it becomes oppressive. If it depends directly (as in Nazi Germany) on race, it is also oppressive. Yet if there is no sense of being a nation at all the whole of society falls apart through incoherence or corruption, and often a dictator emerges intent on making nationality respected by force. Our social order is all the better for being spontaneously created. It is an *evolved organic unity* rooted in place, history, tradition, myth and language. We are not Jacobins or permanent revolutionaries determined to remove or destroy what the past has bequeathed to us. We respect the local, the private, the voluntary, that is to say the intermediate institution. We are not obsessed with individual origins or ancestry and we may be sure that it is only a matter of time before there is a Lord Patel of Leicester, just as there is a Lord Sieff.

Yet such rational objections to the accusations of the anti-racist lobby leave its members unmoved, partly because many of them are driven by a force which is as irrational as real racism. Extreme anti-racists are indeed mirror images of those they are in such a hurry to condemn. They have a similar, missionary urge to cleanse the world of the evil they everywhere profess to see, a similar intolerance and a similar emotional intensity. The question on which this chapter seeks to throw light is why such virulence? For, though there are those of the extreme left who jump on the anti-racist bandwagon because they are looking for a political constituency and a source of recruitment for their cause, most are vehemently sincere.

The vehemence of the anti-racist lobby and the genuine response it arouses from the public derive from three potent, even traumatic experiences in our nation's past and the way we have interpreted or misinterpreted them. They are, first, the horrors perpetrated in the name of a truly racist ideology by our Nazi enemy during the Second World War, above all the holocaust, that is, the murder of six million Jews. For years, to identify someone as racist was to associate them with the unspeakable cruelties of Hitler's SS. Second, our history as the creator and then disbander of a colonial empire has influenced people in two ways. For those who took pride either in the powerful empire which made us a world power or in the Commonwealth (which in some eyes gave us

the moral leadership of the world), the word racist was an insult to our nation's claim to impartial government. On the other hand, those who regarded Britain's colonialism as a long tale of slavery, oppression and exploitation for which we must now make amends, associated the word 'racist' with 'reactionary'. It identified the person so described as one who wished to return to what the left at least considered the most disgraceful episode in our national history. The former 'patriotic' detestation of racism was most influential in the period immediately after the Second World War, while the latter 'anti-British', and normally left-wing, influence prevailed among anti-racists in more recent times.

The third factor, which has facilitated the growth of anti-racism in Britain, was post-war immigration. This caused many ordinary people who were directly affected to give expression to their dismay, which in turn prompted those whose views had already been formed by their interpretation of the other two experiences vehemently to condemn such utterances.

Turning first to Nazism, this evil creed was from the first overtly racist. Its rationale was a bogus theory of the Germans being a superior Aryan race, a *herrenvolk* destined to lord it over the other peoples of the earth, whom they were to conquer and rule. According to this theory the Jews were a sub-human species, responsible for all the ills of German society, who had above all brought about Germany's defeat in the Great War by stabbing her in the back. Such nonsense was pure scapegoatism and scientifically and historically a contemptible myth. There was no biological basis for the idea of a pure Aryan race; the Germans, like all the other peoples of Europe, had a hopelessly mixed mongrel origin and Hitler himself was hardly an example of the blond superman. In any case the Aryan idea was based not on biology but on linguistics. Far from being the enemies of the Fatherland the German Jews, who were a small minority, were particularly well integrated into German society. They were proud to serve in the Kaiser's army and those who emigrated to America continued to associate with other members of the German community over there, in marked contrast with the Jews from other parts of mainland Europe such as Poland and Russia who, once they arrived in the USA, generally had no more to do with other members of the host nation they had left.

The German Jews' patriotism did not however save them from

persecution when the Nazis came to power. Those who were not put into concentration camps fled abroad. Many came to Britain, where it must be said, mainly as a result of a much-resented previous immigration of Jews from eastern Europe fleeing the pogroms of Tsarist Russia and Poland before the Great War, there was a good deal of anti-Semitism. It was found in mild form in a number of popular writers of the time like G.K. Chesterton, Hilaire Belloc and even John Buchan. Nevertheless efforts were made on their behalf. As early as 1933, a fund was opened to place academic refugees in British universities. City bankers were moved to anger by the imprisonment of a Rothschild in Vienna. When the world-famous psychiatrist, Sigmund Freud, arrived in Britain red tape was pushed aside to make him a British citizen and the membership register of the Royal Society, which had never left the society's premises before, was taken to Freud's house for signature. As the historian A.J.P. Taylor put it, 'Nazi treatment of the Jews did more than anything else to turn English moral feeling against Germany.'[2] In the Cambridge Union, the students' debating society, it became a convention that one never told jokes about the Jews, reflecting the feeling that there was nothing funny about people who were being persecuted because of their race. (On one occasion this convention was sorely tried. There was a debate on the situation in Palestine, then part of the British Empire, where the British authorities were being supported against Arab extremists by a Jewish battalion. The Zionist speaker waxed lyrical about the unit's fighting spirit indicated by its motto, 'Charge, charge and charge again'. The members held their breath until relief came when a wit on the other side of the house asked on a point of information whether the speaker wasn't mistaken and the actual motto 'No advance without security'.)

It is a matter of record that the British then and later showed themselves less race-prejudiced than many other nations. They continued to welcome Jewish (and other) refugees during the war, save for a brief period just after the fall of France. This was in marked contrast to the governments of the USA and of the Commonwealth countries, Australia, New Zealand, Canada and especially South Africa, which were particularly restrictive towards Jews.[3]

It is worth noting, incidentally, that the wartime British showed no animosity towards coloured servicemen either, for there is no tradition of hostility against coloured people anywhere in Britain as there is for instance in the southern states of America. Tom Hastie tells a story of how he and a fellow sergeant were stopped in a street in Tunis in 1943 by three black GIs who asked them to be the first to drink from a bottle of brandy they had just bought because they wanted, through them, to thank the British people who had been so good to them. 'They treated us real nice, just like we was their own folks,' said their spokesman.[4]

Those who were old enough at the time to appreciate it will remember the mind-numbing quality of the news of what our soldiers found at Belsen and the further appalling revelations about the systematic murder of millions there and at other camps like Auschwitz and Dachau. We knew that the Nazis were evil but nothing had prepared us for evil on quite this scale. The Nuremberg trials and the capture of a mass of Nazi state documents not only spelt out in horrifying detail how Hitler's minions had carried out these barbaric crimes. They also showed that two million Russian prisoners of war died during captivity and that the Germans had seven and a half million slave labourers from the occupied lands. Furthermore it appeared that this was only the start and that the Nazis had plans for the murder or sterilization of millions more Slavs in order to make room for colonies of the German 'master race'.[5]

There is no truth in the argument that these excesses were due to Germany's being engaged in a life-or-death struggle, for they actually drained resources from the war effort. Had the Germans decided to treat the people in the conquered lands of the East like human beings instead of biological inferiors they might well have succeeded in conquering Russia: when they first arrived in parts of the Ukraine they were welcomed as liberators. The main difference the war made was that it rendered mass slaughter logistically feasible through the acquisition of vast depopulated territories in the East where the process of extermination could be carried out. But there is strong evidence that the Nazis had been planning genocide for the Jews as early as 1927.[6]

It is understandable that faced with this appalling record, many should conclude that racism is the most evil of all types of fanaticism. The left especially has been drawn to this view, and sadly some have sought to monopolize the moral indignation generally felt over the holocaust and to use it for their own ends.

Thus, for instance, an ILEA teaching pack on Auschwitz contains a discussion of Neo-Nazis in the modern world in which, as Caroline Cox has pointed out, there are clear implications that the British action in the Falklands War is to be condemned as unequivocally as the murderous activities of the Nazis.[7] There is assuredly a certain readiness on the left to identify their opponents, such as the Conservatives and upholders of the capitalist system, with the Nazis or fascists. This absurd distortion is due to the fact that their view of the matter is highly selective. They overlook or prefer to forget that 'Nazi' was another word for 'National Socialist' and that the instrument for carrying out genocide was the big, powerful interfering state. They also forget that the Nazis have not been monopolists in genocide.

For refutation of the idea that as mass despatchers of human-kind the Nazis were unique we have only to turn to the Soviet Union, which was engaged in eliminating the so-called Kulaks, that is farmers opposed to collectivization, and in the great Communist party purges, when the Nazis' scheme was only at the planning stage. It was also on a larger scale: to revise the Old Testament dictum, Hitler killed his millions and Stalin his tens of millions. Again, in the course of his 'land reform' in the early 1950s, China's Mao Tse Tung may have executed as many as fifteen million 'counter-revolutionaries'.[8] In relation to population the worst record of all is held by the Khmer Rouge, the Communist regime in Cambodia led by Pol Pot, who without warning drove the town-dwellers into the countryside, so rightly dubbed the killing fields, in the midst of a blazing summer. As a result about a third of them died.[9]

It now appears that the Western aid which went to help the starving in Ethiopia as a result of the generous campaign by Bob Geldof and others, though it did stop many thousands dying from famine, was also used for 'rural resettlement' – in other words forced collectivization and removal from one part of the country to another. In the process, according to the French charity Médecins Sans Frontières one fifth of the half-million people exposed to this treatment died. When the programme is applied to all thirty-five million of the country's farmers it is feared that what happened in Cambodia will be repeated, only on a larger scale.[10]

Most of these operations have been carried out not in the name of race but of socialism. There are, however, examples of racial

21

persecution by Communist regimes. Stalin uprooted the Tartars from their Crimean homeland and resettled them in other parts of the USSR, allegedly as a punishment for collaborating with the German invaders during the war. Although they were rehabilitated in 1967 they have still not been allowed to return.[11]

The oppression of the people of South Vietnam by the victorious Communist Hanoi regime led, as is well known, to the flight of the boat people, most of them in leaky vessels unfit for the high seas, many of which foundered. What is less widely realized is that, of the million or so who thus risked their lives to get away, seventy per cent were ethnically Chinese.[12]

Many will feel that it is unfair by implication to associate Britain's socialists with the Khmer Rouge. But it is equally unfair to lump ordinary British patriots and anti-anti-racists with the Nazis. Indeed there *are* some links between the Khmer Rouge and the far left in Britain, whereas Britain's patriots were for a time the only opponents of Nazi Germany. Those who are now so vocally 'anti-Nazi' are the political descendants of those who supported the Molotov/Ribbentrop pact and called our finest hour 'an Imperialist war'.

The second influence which provides the emotional fuel of anti-racism is an attitude of guilt towards Britain's imperial past. It is summed up in the word 'colonialist' to describe what is alleged to have been an exploitative relationship with the subject countries. Much is made of the earlier period when slaves were shipped across the Atlantic in inhuman conditions. Yet this is an unbalanced indictment which ignores the fact that British idealists, like Granville Sharpe and William Wilberforce, ran a successful campaign against slavery. This led first to the famous test case of 1772 in which Lord Mansfield declared slavery to be incompatible with English common law. As a result 15,000 negroes living in England were set free and subsequently assimilated into the native British population. The slave trade was abolished in 1807, and slavery in British overseas possessions abolished in 1833, at no small cost to the British taxpayer who footed the bill for compensating slave-owners for the loss of their property.

It is none the less often suggested that we should compensate the present descendants of slaves for the injustices suffered by their ancestors. Yet as Thomas Sowell has pointed out, in the case of American blacks, if the principle of compensation is to make up for the difference in the standard of living due to being transferred from Africa to the USA, 'the grotesque conclusion of this arithmetic might be that the blacks pay whites compensation'.[13]

More often it is argued that Britain and other ex-colonial powers have extracted the wealth of the colonies and should now pay it back in the form of financial and technical aid or raising the value of exports through price-support schemes for primary products. This theory of imperialism is, however, based on the fallacious notion that all forms of trade are a zero-sum game, that is to say no trading partner can gain except at the expense of another. In fact most trade is mutually beneficial and, as Adam Smith pointed out long ago, when allied to a free economic order in which people specialize in the economic activities they are best at, creates the wealth of nations. That is why the Third World countries which have had the greatest amount of economic contact with the West in the past are now the most prosperous. Singapore and Malaysia, when discovered by the West, were largely uninhabited jungle and swamp interspersed with a few fishing villages. British enterprise, including the introduction of the rubber-planting, created the foundations of their present flourishing economies. At the other end of the scale countries like Ethiopia, which have had little connection with the West (except for five years of colonial rule under Mussolini), have remained wretchedly poor. Again, the belief that the colonial powers grew rich simply by plundering the colonies assorts oddly with the fact that the richest countries in Europe, Sweden and Switzerland, have never had colonies at all.[14]

A further inconsistency in the doctrine of imperialism as the source of Third-World ills, is the widespread failure to accept that there is effectively only one European empire left in the world – the Russian one. Such a failure may generously be ascribed to the tendency to assume that colonies are only to be found overseas, yet even that excuse has been undermined since the Russians started further-flung imperialist ventures by creating puppet states in Angola and Ethiopia and for a time Mozambique, and client states in Cuba, Nicaragua and Vietnam – the latter with the naval base of Cam Ranh Bay, a touch of real old-fashioned imperialism.

In truth the worst legacy of British colonialism is that of its last phase, the period of the imperial government's war- and post-war socialism. Prior to that British rule in the colonies had been for the most part light, economical and *laissez-faire*. It was reluctant to interfere with the customs of the subject peoples and left the native chieftains as far as possible to enjoy their traditional authority. With the Second World War, export licensing was introduced and other controls followed in their wake. Export monopolies and marketing boards were established for major export crops and, though ostensibly intended to stabilize violent price fluctuations, became the means of exacting heavy taxes. The proceeds were spent on more education and welfare, but these funds laid the basis of post-independence totalitarian states, like Ghana. The *dirigiste* breed of civil servants who were in control during the imperial sunset encouraged the advance not of the traditional and tribal leaders, but of the urbanized, articulate, professional politicians who were to take control with the coming of independence. Many of these leaders had little capacity for government and under them their countries grew poorer. What they mostly did have was the gift of the gab, and in the United Nations they found a ready forum for expounding the thesis, formulated not only by Marxist intellectuals but by a whole body of Western development economists, that the impoverishment of their own countries was due to the depredations of their former colonial masters or, in more updated versions, to the subtler imperialism of Western banks and multinational firms.

The cures advocated for the economic bankruptcy which many of these countries have brought upon themselves are various forms of continuing Western aid. Yet such aid, which goes to governments, and its redistribution effect, as Lord Bauer has classically remarked, are tantamount to taking money from the poor in Western countries to give to the rich in the Third World. Besides, what is not simply pocketed by corrupt politicians and officials is often used to bolster manifestly harmful socialist policies, such as farm collectivization (like that in Tanzania and now, even worse, in Ethiopia), and otherwise undermine the incentives to economic advance.

The third propellant behind the rapid growth of anti-racism has been post-war immigration, mainly from the West Indies and the Indian sub-continent, which has brought the coloured minority to five per cent of the total population. Broadly, the response of the native British to the new arrivals has varied according to their number. While the numbers were low the resentment was muted. When the numbers rose and threatened to go higher still there was resentment by many immediately affected and vague unease among the rest. There was rather less animus against post-war immigrants, as far as one can judge from historians' accounts, than against the Irish who came across St George's Channel during and after Ireland's potato famine last century. The crucial factor then as much as in recent times was numbers. At the height of the famine, three hundred thousand Irish passed in one year through the port of Liverpool alone. The native Britons looked at them askance. One source of prejudice was their Catholicism. They were also shunned, quite reasonably in fact, as bringers of disease and, though it is a myth that they built the railways (they were never more than a third of the labour force involved), they were cordially detested by the Scottish and English navvies with whom they competed for jobs and with whom they often had pitched battles. The Stockport riots of 1852, which began when an English mob attacked an Irish-Catholic procession, were among the worst civil disturbances of the nineteenth century.[15]

Let us look at the numbers of immigrants entering the country in the post-war years. In the period 1946–51 460,000 foreigners came to Britain. The largest group, 115,000, was Polish, men who had served alongside our forces during the war and who did not want to return to a homeland under Stalin's heel, despite the Labour prime minister's appeal to them to do so. The Communists, who then had some MPs at Westminster, were very keen to repatriate them, feeling no doubt that it was perverse of them to turn down the opportunity of living in an egalitarian society. In the event they were retrained under a resettlement scheme and, with the help of a labour shortage, swiftly absorbed into the rest of the population.

Some prisoners of war, Germans, Italians and Ukrainians, were also allowed to settle in Britain. Additionally some European voluntary workers were recruited, mostly from refugee camps in Germany, to work here, though under rather stringent conditions. Although there was a high demand for their labour during the post-war boom there was great hostility to these newcomers on the shop floor. There were also several thousand soldiers and seamen from the West Indies and India who had served in Britain during the war, who decided to stay and work and who were generally made welcome. However, such immigration began only slowly, starting with the arrival of the *Empire Windrush* ship at Tilbury in 1948 with 492 immigrants from Jamaica. The numbers coming in from the West Indies gradually rose to reach an annual rate of 30,000 in 1955 and 1956. They jumped to 98,000 between the beginning of 1961 and the middle of 1962 when there was a rush to beat the Commonwealth Immigrants Act which then came into force, although by then the Asians from the Indian sub-continent were becoming more numerous and the exodus from the West Indies was petering out. Between 1955 and 1968 the total net immigration from the West Indies was 669,640. From then until 1977 318,521 settled here, but as a result of increasing restrictions about four-fifths of those were dependants. By 1984 the total immigration had shrunk and that from the New Commonwealth countries was down to 24,800.[16] (These are of course official figures and do not allow for those who came in illegally.)

The response to this immigration revealed a startling gap between the politicians and the people. The alarm in the constituencies, especially those, in order of importance, in the South East, the Midlands, the North and the North West, for the most part found little echo in Westminster. A Tory minister for the colonies, Henry Hopkinson, was still proclaiming at the end of 1954 that Commonwealth citizens of any colour could say 'Civis Romanus sum' and come freely to the mother country. The well-to-do progressive Tory MP Humphry Berkeley, when asked if he would like to live in a coloured area, used to say that he already had coloured neighbours – he lived next door to the Indian ambassador.

What brought people and politicians closer together was, inevitably, the latter's need of the former's votes. Some, like Paul Foot in his entertaining study *Immigration and Race in British Politics,*[17] regarded this conjunction as a shameful surrender to vulgar prejudice and xenophobia. But was it? A comprehensive survey conducted by the Institute of Race Relations[18] and published in 1969 indicated that the attitudes of the British public towards race relations were pretty rational. Nearly three quarters of them were 'tolerant-inclined' and only ten per cent were strongly prejudiced against coloured people. Regarding jobs and housing, the majority wanted no discrimination between white and coloured people and those who did want it were invariably the ones who were directly threatened themselves. The survey did point to an apparent irrationality of the majority who thought that the immigrants were taking more out of the country than they were putting in – irrational because the immigrants' lifespan in Britain included a higher proportion of time working and therefore contributing to the economy than the British-born. Yet the view was not completely groundless, for in the short term any considerable influx, especially if concentrated in one area, was bound to put a strain on local health, education, police and other services.

The eventual introduction of restrictions on immigration was entirely sensible as a means of avoiding social disruption resulting from the attempt to digest too many people of alien ways at one time. That they were adopted despite the opposition of most politicians is nothing to be ashamed of but should be seen as a vindication of our democratic system. Yet the conversion of political pooh-bahs was slow. The empire men in the Tory party, the Commonwealth enthusiasts in the Labour party and the radicals on both sides who didn't want to touch anything remotely connected with racial prejudice, for a long time avoided any action to stem the rising immigrant tide. When forced by public pressure to take the first faltering step in restriction in 1961 it was with great reluctance. In the wake of restriction came a quango, known first as the Race Relations Board and later the Commission for Racial Equality, to monitor racial prejudice and bring the more obstinate offenders to court. These bodies could almost be called the revenge which establishment politicians took on the voters for making them bring in immigration controls against their will. In the process, as we shall see, they gave authority to people who had every interest in opposing such controls. For, if race frictions were reduced by such limits on the entry of immigrants, the services of the race relations industry would be in less demand.

It was this feeling that Britain's politicians were failing to provide against a major preventible social problem that caused Enoch Powell to make a speech in Birmingham on 20 April 1968 on the subject of race relations which shattered the complacency of the political establishment. He dwelt on the fears of many whites of becoming a minority in their own land. He spoke of how the number of immigrants, instead of diminishing, would grow so fast that it would not be possible to integrate them. (This proposition, incidentally, shows how far removed he was from being racist, for what racist believes in integration?) Under existing policies, he said, it was like watching the nation building its own funeral pyre. To bring in legislation at this juncture, as Parliament proposed, in order to punish discrimination, was to 'risk throwing a match on to gunpowder'. He urged the adoption of a policy of voluntary repatriation before it was too late. He was filled with foreboding and like the Roman seemed to see 'the River Tiber foaming with much blood' – a prophecy that was in some measure to be fulfilled in the later riots in Bristol, Brixton, Tottenham, Handsworth and Toxteth.[19]

The speech was swiftly disowned by his leader, Edward Heath, not because it was against Conservative party policy but because of its tone. Powell was dismissed from the shadow cabinet at the same time. In the country at large however he became for the majority something of a hero. Letters of support poured in by the sackful. London dockers lobbied their Labour MPs on behalf of Powell. An opinion poll showed that 74 per cent of the sample had agreed with the speech and 69 per cent thought Heath wrong to dismiss him.

The Birmingham speech was a milestone because it brought a matter of supreme concern for many ordinary citizens, which most of their representatives had tacitly conspired to ignore, into the mainstream of party politics. Had it not done so, popular frustrations might well have been enlisted in support of uglier activists, members of the National Front and people of that ilk, who dwell on the sleazy sidelines of the political debate. The country remains in Powell's debt for having refused to submit to the race relations lobby and for so forthrightly repudiating its insistent doctrine that racism is institutionalized in the British way of life. As this chapter has sought to show, by ordinary and comparative as opposed to ideal standards, there is nothing shameful in Britain's handling of the great post-war immigration boom except the failure of our politicians to act in time to limit the social damage caused by its becoming too large comfortably to contain. Indeed, by almost any contemporary or historical comparison, our record of absorbing immigrants has been a remarkable success.

3

Race Discrimination, the Quango Non-Cure

Without government sponsorship the race relations industry, like many other largely nationalized concerns, would scarcely exist. So, in chronicling its rise, we have to trace the legislative steps in 1965, 1968 and 1976 which established the core of institutions through which it aims to transform British society. Though the purpose of its authors has not wavered, the organizational picture has lost focus through a bewildering change of names. The Race Relations Board, with which the attempt of government to supervise relations between the races began, was later supplemented by the Community Relations Commission. These two bodies were then merged into the Commission for Racial Equality to which, at local level, Community Relations Councils were linked. Before burrowing into these complexities it is worth reflecting on the revolution such laws and institutions entailed.

In Britain's long history of receiving immigrants this was the first time that the authorities had been involved in regulating the way the native population behaved towards them. There was, admittedly, one precedent for UK legislation against racial discrimination in the Government of India Act 1833 which provided that no one should be denied employment in the Indian Civil Service solely because of his race or colour. However, though this was a British statute, its application was to India.[1] In the past Jews, Flemings, French Huguenots, Irish and many other peoples had arrived and settled without any laws being passed to protect them or supervisory body created to watch over them. Indeed there was some legislating discrimination *against* them such as the Test Act, which kept Jews out of Parliament, though this was not technically racial since it applied to Catholics and Nonconformists as well. But in general the assumption was that the same law applied equally to all. The liberal state was one in which the laws were few and the ideal, in Locke's words, was that they should be known and certain and not subject to arbitrary individual whim. Samuel Johnson expressed the prevailing scepticism of what law and government could achieve in the lines he added to Goldsmith's 'Traveller':

> How small, of all that human hearts endure,
> That part which laws or kings can cause or cure!

That was before today's big state which rests on the conviction that any problem can be solved by the right kind of law. For most people in Britain today have lived most of their lives under governments which have encouraged the belief that for almost every problem there is a political solution. That is why MPs still groan and grow old before their time under the sheer weight of statutes they are obliged to push through the parliamentary mill. To deal with the consequent increase in regulation, the civil servants (at least until Mrs Thatcher arrived in Number 10) have bred and the judges have multiplied. Yet even this growth in control and supervision could not satisfy the legislative urge of Britain's post-war socialist governments. In addition to laws intended to reform they created supplementary institutions to supervise the enforcement of such laws. These bodies were called quangos, an acronym for quasi-autonomous non-governmental organizations. Their growth under post-war Labour governments was something wonderful to behold.

The statutory race relations organizations were classic quangos. Their growth was classic too. Their beginnings were modest, amounting in the first instance to little more than an exercise in gesture politics; but then they proceeded to expand, largely by fostering demand for their services among the pressure groups. There has doubtless been an element of conspiracy, but their expansion is better viewed as the kind of development which is almost inevitable when sectional interests are allowed to establish themselves inside the government machine.

Their emergence in the swinging sixties was symbolic of a moral sea-change in the nation's affairs. The English, even in the days of minimal government, were not loath to regulate sin, including gambling, drunkenness and above all sex. But, in the traditional catalogue of vice, racism was not to be found. On the contrary it was fashionable in the period before the Great War to express patriotic sentiments in terms of race (though only a few took this seriously as a biological theory); there was no question, for instance, of prosecuting Rudyard Kipling when he wrote his 'Recessional' about 'lesser breeds without the law'.

It is significant that in the sixties major moves towards sexual permissiveness and the first statutory penalty laid down for racism should coincide. Racism is by no means peculiar to our era, but it is surely more of an obsession and a source of guilt in our time than at any other in history. This conjunction of diminishing condemnation of sexual misbehaviour or deviance and increased censoriousness and readiness to penalize words or actions based on racial bias was overseen and to an extent fostered by Roy Jenkins, Home Secretary when most of these changes took place.

An ardent admirer, indeed biographer, of H.H. Asquith, Roy Jenkins was less a socialist than a latter-day version, reincarnation almost, of the nineteenth-century Liberal reformer, except that he promoted some very unVictorian reforms. With the same rather self-righteous zeal which his spiritual forbears brought to measures for the improvement of the masses he swept aside a whole battery of state-imposed restraints on sexual morals. He introduced easier divorce by conniving at private members' bills, legalized abortion and removed penalties for homosexual acts in private between consenting adults and over the live theatre ended the Lord Chamberlain's control. At the same time this rather stuffy and unlikely apostle of sexual liberation blazed the coercive trail to racial harmony, which he defined 'not as a flattening process of assimilation, but as equal opportunity accompanied by cultural diversity, in an atmosphere of mutual tolerance'. Quite why he considered the natural and spontaneous process of assimilation to be by implication more 'flattening' than legislation imposed and enforced by the mighty bureaucratic apparatus of the state is a mystery. His biographer argues that Jenkins was concerned for Britain's image in the world and took a strongly positive view of the contribution that Commonwealth immigrants, like previous

31

waves of immigrants from the Norman Conquest to the refugees of the thirties, could make in overcoming 'our natural island lethargy'.[2] In the Jenkins view of things, immigration was good for Britain and if people resisted it they should be socially engineered into accepting it. It is not surprising that already, even among his colleagues, the impression was growing that his liberalism bore an arrogant taint. 'Despite all his care,' Barbara Castle noted in her diary, 'his instinctive high-handedness will slip out.'[3]

The first statutory step in obligatory integration in 1965, however, owed less to Jenkins than to expediency. Labour, which had won the 1964 general election with a wafer-thin parliamentary majority, was attempting to project an image of purpose in power while pandering to every interest whose opposition might later rob them of office. Happily for them, their Prime Minister was one of the great survivors of all time, who delighted in setting up enquiries and inventing new committees which, as he once remarked, 'takes minutes and wastes years'.

Labour had taken up a holier-than-thou attitude to the immigration controls introduced by the Tories in 1961. Hugh Gaitskell, leader of the Labour party at the time, denounced the Tory proposals as a 'miserable, shabby, shameful bill'. Barbara Castle condemned it for violating the Commonwealth idea of the free flow of traffic and insisted that Labour would 'get rid of control altogether'.[4] That approach didn't last long however as the reactions came in from the constituencies. After Harold Wilson succeeded Gaitskell as Labour leader, following the former's sudden death, he accepted that there would have to be controls but took refuge in a formula, which in effect was no more than a fudge, for agreeing restraints on immigration with other Commonwealth governments. In fact the controls were not effective enough and there was growing concern in those areas, especially the West Midlands, where the concentration of immigrants was most intense.

The general election result in 1964 was ominous and revealing. In the midst of a Labour victory one result stood out like a sore thumb – the gain of Smethwick by the Tory, Peter Griffiths, at the expense of Labour's Patrick Gordon Walker, who had represented the constituency for nineteen years. There is little doubt that Griffiths won on the immigration issue and had been able to make much of the fact that Gordon Walker had led the Labour party's attack on the Tory immigration control measures in 1961. Wilson became very indignant about this in the House of Commons and castigated Griffiths as a 'parliamentary leper'. It was an exercise in sheer humbug, as shown by the fact that soon afterwards Wilson began implementing the policy of tighter controls for which Griffiths had campaigned. The consultation with the New Commonwealth countries predictably proved a farce, Maurice Foley, whom Wilson had put in charge of immigrants' affairs, reporting to him that a huge increase in immigration levels was expected. Wilson cut back the number of work vouchers issued under the 1962 Act and, as far as dependants were concerned, reduced the qualifying range.

The Labour leader was by temperament less a political prophet than a fixer. He realized how important it was psychologically for Labour to feel superior to their opponents on the issue of race. Having had to bow to public demand for immigration controls, it was necessary to refurbish their moral credentials in some politically less damaging way. For this reason Wilson issued a White Paper promising a law against incitement to race hatred and the prohibition of racial discrimination.

Such a proposal had already been put forward year after year in a private member's bill by a genuine idealist and anti-colonialist campaigner, Fenner Brockway. It must have given many pause for thought that he, like Gordon Walker, had lost his seat at Eton and Slough, near London, in the 1964 election. According to his autobiography[5] this was due partly to lack of enthusiasm for his stand on race in the local Labour party. It didn't help that his most prominent contribution to debates in the House of Commons was on colonial issues which made some of his constituents think that he cared more about the rights of people overseas (increasing numbers of whom were arriving in Slough looking for jobs) than about those who sent him to Westminster. As he says, 'Only on polling day itself did I learn that in one of the biggest wards, no election committee had functioned because the secretary did not like my views on race.' He himself had no doubt that the determining issue was the arrival in Slough of large numbers of Commonwealth immigrants, though there was no question in this instance, as there had been at Smethwick, of the Tory candidate, Sir Anthony Meyer, playing the race card. It would be truer to say that it played itself.

33

Following, then, the pattern of the Brockway bills the government's Race Relations Bill proposed to make racial discrimination an offence punishable by a maximum fine of £100 if practised in hotels, public houses, restaurants, theatres, cinemas, public transport and any place of public resort maintained by a public authority. It also made incitement to racial hatred illegal and punishable by up to two years' imprisonment or a maximum fine of £1,000. The Public Order Act 1936 (which had been brought in to deal with the rough-house tactics of Mosley's fascists) was to be extended to cover threatening, abusive or insulting words or behaviour which were likely to cause a breach of the peace.

The incitement to racial hatred part of the bill was not controversial. As a matter of fact it was due less to racist propaganda against coloured people than to anti-Semitic speeches at public meetings in the early 1960s. This change in the law was strongly urged by the Board of Deputies of British Jews.

More disputatious was the proposal to make racial discrimination in public places a criminal offence. The Conservatives opposed this, preferring a policy of conciliation. Perhaps because this approach was also supported by the Campaign Against Racial Discrimination and the Labour lawyers, the government modified its bill. In the new draft, in order to secure compliance with the anti-discrimination provisions, the Race Relations Board was conceived, though its actual birth was attended by complications.

It is hard to believe that Harold Wilson saw the Race Relations Act which then passed with opposition support as anything more than a very useful public relations exercise. Honour was satisfied, the lobbies, chattering classes and even the Tories were placated. At the same time the act's limited range of application should mean that it would not upset the all-important average voter, and what resentment did occur could be absorbed by the Race Relations Board, leaving the government unscathed.

Its main merit was as a safety-valve. That was how the Home Secretary, Sir Frank Soskice, who had guided it through its various stages, evidently saw it. Summing up he said: 'We have taken what in a sense is a first step. I hope that events will show that it is not necessary to take any further step and that this may be the last step. If the bill turns out to be a successful Act of Parliament and to achieve its purpose, it will, by a paradox . . . very rarely need to be called into operation.' It would, he reflected, be 'an ugly day in

34

this country' if they had to come back to Parliament to extend the legislation's scope.

Alas for Sir Frank's optimism! That 'ugly day' was to come far sooner than he expected. He reckoned without the growth potential of all bureaucracies whenever they're given the chance. He also, to amend a phrase of Walt Whitman's, overlooked 'the infinite audacity of unelected men', especially the race relations pressure groups, who were already planning to expand the functions of the board far beyond what Sir Frank had envisaged. Another factor was his own ill-health, which meant that he soon resigned and his place as Home Secretary was taken by Roy Jenkins, a great admirer of the Kennedy/Johnson administrations' affirmative action approach to racial affairs, which admittedly was not then so evidently the disaster it later became.

The original idea had been to appoint an obviously independent chairman to the Race Relations Board, partly to counterbalance the other two members, Sir Learie Constantine, the famous former West Indian cricketer, and Dr Joost de Blank, former Archbishop of Cape Town and apartheid campaigner. For both these gentlemen, however eminent, were too much cast in the role of crusaders to be considered wholly impartial. The trouble was that, to start with at least, nobody of stature wanted to take the top job. It was turned down both by Lord Selkirk and Kenneth Younger. Jenkins solved the problem by appointing an old Oxford friend, Mark Bonham-Carter, a well-connected Liberal (brother-in-law of Jo Grimond, the Liberal leader, and grandson of H.H. Asquith), who had recently lost his seat.

By the time Bonham-Carter took over Dr Joost de Blank had resigned and Mr B.S. Langton, former Mayor of Manchester, had been appointed in his place. He and Sir Learie were only part-timers. Bonham-Carter's salary was only £4,000 a year and the modesty of the establishment was shown by the fact that it did not qualify for a switchboard. The annual bill for salaries, fees and other expenses for the whole organization was only £35,000. The race relations lobbies, however, were determined that it should not stay that way. One of the more ominous developments was that the Campaign Against Racial Discrimination (CARD) was planning to form groups to uncover cases of discrimination and to open a complaints office with white volunteers ready to apply for houses and jobs refused to coloured applicants. This *agent provocateur* activism was far removed from the minimal interference hoped for by Sir Frank Soskice when he summed up the debate on the third reading of the act.

There seems little doubt that Jenkins and Bonham-Carter thenceforth co-operated with the pressure groups to extend the functions and powers of the board. Both the board and the National Committee for Commonwealth Immigrants (set up under the chairmanship of the Archbishop of Canterbury on 1 April 1964) produced reports in 1967 calling for an extension of the anti-discrimination law to other fields, including housing, employment, home loans and insurance. They then jointly financed research by Political and Economic Planning which did a sample survey in six cities and reached similar conclusions. These were further supported by a group of lawyers in the Street Report, also financed by the board and national committee.

It is fascinating that the survey of Race Relations, which contained a careful investigation by Research Services Limited showing, broadly, how tolerant the British people were towards immigrants, had its preliminary results appear only after the second Race Relations Bill was published and only just in time for the Commons debate. For by that time, since the government had decided to back it, the legislation was a *fait accompli*. In the survey a nationwide sample showed that a large majority were against discrimination on grounds of colour in the most vital areas of jobs and housing. Further, colour prejudice in general was found to be lower among the younger than the older age groups, a hopeful sign for the future. This hardly squared with the conclusion of the PEP Report – that there was substantial discrimination against coloured people – one of the two pillars which supported Jenkins' case for having the bill at all.

Although the draft bill had been drawn up at the Home Office under Roy Jenkins, his departure for the Treasury meant that the task of pushing it through the Commons fell to his successor, James Callaghan, who did not have quite the same enthusiasm for its aims. The bill, though it duly got through, had by no means a trouble-free passage. For one thing it had been preceded two months before by something approaching a panic measure to control immigration of East African Asians, large numbers of whom, after independence in Kenya, Uganda and Tanzania, were found to have the right to passports letting them enter Britain, and likely to make use of that right owing to persecution by their governments. Certainly the number of Commonwealth immigrants had risen sharply, from 63,211 in 1965 to 74,977 in 1967 (Home Office statistics). As a result the bill looked like a sop to liberal opinion to compensate for surrendering to popular clamour for further immigration control. Moreover Enoch Powell had made his controversial Birmingham speech three days before the Commons debate.

The act which finally emerged made racial discrimination in housing, employment and services such as insurance and credit facilities illegal. It also banned the 'no coloureds' kind of advertisement and made it illegal for a hotel-keeper to refuse a room on racial grounds. The Race Relations Board was to be enlarged – its existing £60,000 grant was trebled – and there was to be an additional body, the Community Relations Commission, to concentrate on fostering racial harmony and to advise and make recommendations to the Home Secretary on matters affecting community relations. Mark Bonham-Carter, who had earlier complained that the board was not empowered to act on one in five of the complaints that it received, had now obtained the additional role, powers and staff for which he had campaigned.

All the extra bodies were soon required to deal with a veritable torrent of complaints from people claiming to be victims of racial discrimination. Did this show how much the changes were needed? There is little reason to think so. First, there is the elementary point that where there is a demand for a commodity or service, the market will supply it: this applies to complaints of racial discrimination as much as it does to hamburgers. Second, many of the complaints were time-wasting and absurd, which suggests that genuine complaints were in short supply.

One of the incidents early reported to the board concerned a country-inn landlord in Cambridge, a ripe character John Hollick de la Taste Tickell. He was locally known as 'the squire of Whittlesford', a village in Cambridgeshire, and wore eighteenth-century knee breeches behind the bar of his pub, the Tickell Arms. He had a row with a coloured student during Cambridge university's May Week, when a Trinidadian accompanied by a white girl from Homerton training college came in too late to be served lunch. In the altercation that followed, Tickell, according to his own account, said that if the chap didn't like the way

England was run he could go back to his own country – 'But this was no more than I would have told a Scotsman or an Australian in similar circumstances.' Tickell continued:

I am a fervent supporter of Enoch Powell, but this remark certainly had nothing to do with the colour of the student's skin. Why, I've even danced with Princess Elizabeth of Toro [Uganda's first woman barrister] at a party given by Lord Birdwood. And you can't get much blacker than she is, the beautiful girl. Fortunately my public house is most popular with the undergraduates – Indians, Africans, Siamese and Chinese come in here. Some have already offered to give evidence on my behalf.[6]

More notorious was the case of an Eastbourne doctor who put an advertisement in *The Times* personal column for a 'Scottish daily help able to do plain cooking including porridge'. The Race Relations Board ruled that it should have read, 'Daily for Scottish family able to do some plain Scottish cooking'. This fatuous piece of sub-editing was attacked in the House of Commons by the member for Eastbourne, Sir Charles Taylor, who said of the board, 'All these bumptious asses should be removed.' He went on, 'We remember Mr Mark Bonham-Carter, when he sat on the bench behind me, and we realized then that he had little sense of humour.' On reading of the case, Mr Bill Feazey, a butcher in Bexley, Kent, immediately reacted by placing an advertisement in one of his shops for a 'Scottish butcher able to cut Scottish meat', in the hope of being reported to the Race Relations Board so that he could expose how ridiculous it was.[7]

In November 1969 there were complaints about a TV comedy show called 'Curry and Chips' starring Spike Milligan as a Pakistani immigrant, in which there were references to 'coons and wogs'. In this instance, a board official was wary and said he did not think the board should become involved, but it was not the last he was to hear of it.[8] Two months later the issue was raised again by Clive Jenkins, joint General Secretary of the Association of Scientific, Technical and Managerial Staffs. But he was too late: the series had ended on Boxing Day.

Already in the first year of the bill it was becoming apparent how inadequate general rules about racial discrimination often are to deal with the complexities they are designed to regulate. For instance there was the case of a photographer who refused to take coloured clients. The photographer maintained that this was not due to colour prejudice but to the fact that coloured people wanted him to provide extra lighting to make their skins look fairer and at seven shillings and sixpence a time he couldn't afford it.[9] A Pakistani accused of race prejudice because he put a notice reading 'Wanted – English Lodger' in his front window was acquitted when it was found that he wanted an English lodger to teach his five children English.[10]

The board showed its mettle, though, in April 1970 when it moved in swiftly to stop members of Gentleshaw and Cannock Wood Women's Institute in Staffordshire from singing 'Ten Little Nigger Boys' in a talent contest. Nothing daunted the women from the villages near Lichfield substituted 'golliwogs' for 'nigger boys' and won third prize.[11]

The growing number of trivial cases began to worry the board, not as an indication that there might be some basic flaw in the system but because they led to the assumption that no one was taking racial discrimination seriously. And indeed in January 1970 someone played a hoax on firms all over the country, sending them letters with Race Relations Board headed notepaper ordering them gradually to increase their employment of immigrants to twenty-five per cent by 1980, sacking white workers if necessary to achieve this result.[12] Similarly no one was sure whether Wilf Proudfoot, the Tory MP for Brighouse and Spenborough, was being serious or pulling everyone's leg when he complained to the BBC that it provided nineteen hours a week of broadcasting in Welsh compared with only one and a half in Hindi and Urdu, though Britain had far more speakers of the latter two languages than of Welsh. What was the board to do if the English girls at Henley College of Further Education fulfilled their promise of presenting their petition complaining that they were not allowed to wear trousers while the Asians girls were?[13]

Young bachelors could get into trouble too. One such advertised in a Brighton newspaper for 'an attractive girlfriend of European origin'. A complaint was sent to the Race Relations Board by middle-aged Mr Alan Hancock, an engineer of Lower Rock Gardens, Brighton, who claimed that the advertisement contravened the Race Relations Act, but added, 'The effect of my action may be to demonstrate that the act is absurd.'[14]

That was a feeling widely shared. It seemed that the most innocent of transactions could be found to contravene the act and all sorts of simple souls suddenly descended on by race relations officials demanding to know if they realized that they had been breaking the law of the land. In March 1971 Mr Jack Tamburro, an accordionist at the Vineyard Restaurant in Birmingham, advertised for an Italian singer to join a trio. The advertisement said that an English singer would also be considered but there was a complaint that this discriminated against any singer who was not Italian or English. The point was, of course, as a bemused Mr Tamburro made clear, that it didn't really matter what race the person was provided he could sing fluently in Italian.[15]

Why should clanking officialdom ever have got involved in such a minor affair? The old legal motto *De minimis non curat lex* – the law is not concerned with trivia – was something which the race relations industry had never fully grasped. Senior figures at the Race Relations Board continued to be worried about the trivial cases that were arising because they feared that they would bring the law of race relations into disrepute, especially among the immigrant community. What did not seem to have occurred to them was that the absurdity was not the result of mischief but inherent in the race relations law itself. It had been given wide-ranging yet vague jurisdiction over what people had long considered to be an extensive but private realm where only their own personal standards prevailed. If a law is to be effective it must mirror a moral consensus, not impose a standard which the majority rejects. It cannot command respect if it enters a sphere of human activity where most people consider that it has no business to be. A law needs to be precise, so that people know exactly what their obligations are, not blurred, inspirational and brimful of optimism that those over whom it holds sway will have a change of heart or be born again. It was because it did not measure up to such commonsense criteria, because it deserted them for the more alien concepts of law as an auxiliary to a crusade, that the law had become such an ass.

Let us turn for a moment to the Community Relations Commission – the new junior partner for the Race Relations Board created by the 1968 Act. Considering that its task was to foster felicitous relations between the races the appointment as its first chairman of the abrasive Frank Cousins, retiring boss of Britain's largest union, the TGWU, seems in retrospect decidedly strange. Nowadays, after so many years of Mrs Thatcher, we tend to forget what pooh-bahs those old union barons used to be. His official, painstaking biographer, Geoffrey Goodman, suggests the appointment was due to Cousins being 'of course, profoundly committed to fighting racial prejudice'. The only example he offers of this commitment was to do with the London busmen in Cousins' own union, and the details are sparse.[16] Otherwise it was apparently based on the sentiment generated long ago by an Indian doctor who once restored his injured mother. It seems more likely that his was just a routine quango appointment selected from the Labour government's list of the Great and the Good. It might also have owed something to the fact that the job was in the gift of James Callaghan, who was at the time ingratiating himself with the union chiefs whom he was soon afterwards to gratify by blocking Barbara Castle's 'In Place of Strife' scheme for union reform. In any case Cousins was the wrong man for the job. He upset the staff with his imperious ways. He couldn't see why the CRC should be separate from the board and like a typical TGWU boss wanted a merger.

He had no time for a body which was all propaganda and no muscle, and thought that the operation was hopelessly small and underfunded. Yet the accounts for the year 1970 showed that it had underspent its annual allowance of £350,000 by £22,000.

In 1970 Jeff Crawford, a leading figure in the West Indian Standing Committee, wrote to Cousins tactfully suggesting that he should resign on health grounds and give way to a younger man. By November this is what he had done, with Mark Bonham-Carter moving over from the board to fill his place. A few months later a top mandarin, John Burgh, was drafted in as Deputy Chairman.

A still more senior civil servant took Mark Bonham-Carter's vacant chair at the Race Relations Board. This was Sir Geoffrey Wilson, a former Permanent Secretary at the Ministry of Overseas Development, described in *The Times* as a 'bureaucrat's bureaucrat'. With his radical Quaker background and one-time close connection with Labour's most puritanical Chancellor of the Exchequer, Sir Stafford Cripps, he could hardly fail to have acquired a sense of moral superiority which was appropriate to his new job.

41

The arrival of these high-powered functionaries signalled the beginning of a quieter period in the history of the board and the commission. In its annual report published in July 1971 the board was optimistic that, since the numer of complaints received was down from 1,549 to 1,024, the initial surge of racial discrimination complaints had spent itself and that the frivolous ones were at last phasing out. In truth the reduced tempo more probably reflected the change of atmosphere which came with a new government after the Conservatives won the 1970 general election. For the Conservatives, though pledged to further racial harmony, were not especially enamoured of the race quangos (a word not yet in use) and were evidently not going to encourage them in their sillier quests. Indeed, had it not been for the fact that the Race Relations Board had been forced down Edward Heath's throat by the fuss over Enoch Powell, whom he disliked, it might have had a much thinner time.

As it was, the dottier cases did not disappear completely. In December 1971 a London-based company complained that it was investigated by the Race Relations Board because it had advertised for a Scottish chartered accountant. The board was apparently unaware of the fact that a Scottish chartered accountant is an accountant of any nationality who has qualified in Scotland. The managing director of the firm, Mr George Campbell-Johnston, said that the advertisement was aimed at successful candidates in the Scottish Chartered Accountants examination, the results of which had just been published. He described the board's action as 'footling interference likely to breed the very hatred it purports to eradicate'.[17]

The Conservative MP Patrick Wall waxed indignant in the House of Commons about the Race Relations Board's decision to take a Merseyside businessman to court over his refusal to employ an Irishman shortly after the Birmingham pub bombings in 1974. The following spring of 1975 a Welsh solicitor, who was also vice-president of Plaid Cymru, the Welsh Nationalist party, complained to the Race Relations Board about the recent use of the word 'wélshing' by Reg Prentice, Education Minister, which he described as 'blatantly racialist and abusive'. His letter to the board was motivated, he said, by 'strong and very deeply felt resentment'.[18]

Thomas Cook, the travel agent, was the target of another

complaint by an anti-apartheid campaigner for offering holidays in South Africa restricted to whites, though of course, since the South African government was making the rules, the company could offer either those kinds of holidays in South Africa or none at all.[19]

In the eyes of most people such cases indicated that the staff of the Race Relations Board were wholly unrealistic. And if it was the law that was at fault then what kind of a law was it which gratuitously stirred up trouble between the English, Scots, Irish and Welsh? Yet the board, far from relenting, was now engaged, though not very successfully, in pursuing cases of discrimination in private clubs. The board's annual report also invariably demanded that it should have wider powers. Its paternalist tone was unwavering and was particularly noticeable when it argued in its report published in mid-1982 that most victims did not complain because (like Molière's Monsieur Jourdain who had no idea that he was speaking prose) they did not realize that they were suffering discrimination. It was also apparent that the board felt the government was not doing enough about consulting its race relations bodies, on immigration policy for instance, though on that issue many MPs thought it would do better to consult the electors. The constant theme was the demand for more powers. In this respect the most persuasive case was for the discretionary power not to investigate a complaint where in the board's view no useful purpose could be served. This would have avoided the more fatuous publicity-stunt complaints, yet the corollary was that no citizen could then be denied the right to pursue a racial discrimination suit in the courts. That, however, would work against the spirit of the 1965 Act which was trying to minimize racial conflicts by treating them as a public wrong to be settled as far as possible by conciliation. As Sir Frank Soskice had said in the debate when the 1965 legislation was going through, it would be 'a mistake to open the door to individual complaints which could be pressed further and further'.

Other demands for additional powers looked more like empire-building. Arguing that it was better to stop unlawful discrimination before it happened, the board sought authority similar to that of factory inspectors to investigate an establishment on suspicion that the law was being breached. The Home Secretary during the Heath government, Robert Carr, however, thought the board had quite enough power already. His main concern was to avoid provoking a sharp polarization of public opinion. At that time he was busy damping down fears of repatriation of illegal immigrants (brought about by Enoch Powell's campaign) and had instructed chief constables around the country to go easy on the search for them. While this was going on he had no call for a rejigged Race Relations Board stirring the pot and enraging the Tory right, some of whom already saw it as a haven for black-power agitators.

With the collapse of the Heath administration in 1974, the return of Labour to power and the reinstallation of Roy Jenkins in the Home Office, the board's pleas for an increasingly interventionist policy on race had a more sympathetic hearing. The response, though, was not necessarily to the board's taste. The all-party Select Committee of MPs reporting in June 1975 said that the Race Relations Board and the Community Relations Commission had failed and should be scrapped. Alas, this flash of wisdom was brief: the committee sought to put a new, much larger, Equal Rights Commission in their place. (Curiously enough a high-powered Tory committee had earlier recommended something similar to Edward Heath, except that it wanted to retain the board and make it responsible also for women's rights. One joker commented that the suggestion had taken this form because it would be more appealing to testy old bachelor Heath, who viewed women as members of a different race.)

Roy Jenkins went further than any of his predecessors and created an Equal Opportunities Commission, in addition to reshaping the race quangos. In the latter case he followed the recommendation of Lord Rothschild's Central Policy Review Staff, that the Race Relations Board and the Community Relations Commission should be merged. The objection to such a merger was that it would muddle the two functions for which the two bodies stood, mixing up the 'policeman's' role of the board with the educative and fact-finding task of the commission. The reply of the merger enthusiasts was that this was to mistake the role of the policeman, who should be as much concerned with the prevention of crime by the alleviation of its causes as with law enforcement.

So the merger went through and out of the ashes of the Race Relations Board and the Community Relations Commission, there arose, phoenix-like, the Commission for Racial Equality, the whole of which was larger than the two former parts. This was because it had a more ambitious role. The new act prohibited racial discrimination in employment, training, education, housing, the provision of goods, facilities and services and advertising. And the new body acquired machinery similar to that provided in the Sex Discrimination Act for assuring equal opportunities for women.

Meanwhile the flow of immigrants into the country (which had fallen after the Conservative Immigration Act of 1971 from the previous level of 63,000 a year to 34,044 in 1973) was, as a result of certain relaxations, such as the right of Indian women to bring in their fiancés, again on the rise. Estimated to be running at 50,000 a year, all the signs were that the figure was about to increase dramatically. In a Commons debate on the subject in May 1976 Enoch Powell made the shock revelation of an internal report by a Home Office official, Mr Charles Hawley, who had gone to India to assess the waiting lists of dependants applying for entry to Britain. The Labour Minister of State concerned, Alex Lyon, had estimated in 1975 that the waiting list was 180,000, which could disappear in two years. Hawley, however, reported that new applicants were appearing as fast as entry certificates were granted. It was well known that certificates could easily be bought, and, given the Indian joint family system, arranged marriages, and the loose British definition of 'dependant', there was every justification for Powell's comment in the debate (which provoked cries of 'fascist') that 'far from emptying a finite pool' they were 'trying to bail out the ocean'.[20]

4

The Urge to Affirmative Action

One of the sadder stories from the verbal history of our times is the decline in status of the word 'discrimination'. Not so long ago it was a term of approval: a discriminating person was one of superior taste and discernment, one who judged all things and held fast to that which was good. Discrimination in this sense and a class of people cultivated enough to exercise it were perceived as indispensable to civilized society. Alas no longer: to discriminate about almost anything nowadays is to invite angry cries of 'élitist' (unless one is engaged in *positive* discrimination). Which is to say that 'discrimination' is now an abuse word, part of the arsenal of recrimination, an admission of which involves incriminating oneself. Race discrimination stands near the top of the list of latter-day social sins.

Today's discrimination-phobia is surely related to the habit of describing all human differences as 'inequalities'. The effect of this is to pass from recognizing that one thing is not the same as another to a more traumatic situation where any difference is assumed to be bad because it offends against the egalitarian ideal.[1] Yet, 'We cannot avoid every sort of distinction or discrimination. If we set out to establish equality in one respect, we shall establish some other inequality in another respect.'[2] The classic illustration of this is in Communist countries, where the economic inequalities of property-ownership have been exchanged for far greater political inequalities, with life-or-death powers placed in the hands of the Communist party and the secret police. Similarly, though of course far less spectacularly, the suppression of alleged race-based

47

inequalities has called for the establishment of a new inequality of power between the members of the race relations industry and the rest of society, over which its trustee, the Commission for Racial Equality, has obtained novel discretionary power. For, under the Race Relations Act of 1976, the CRE's remit was not only extended to cover employment, education, the provision of goods, services and property. It was also authorized formally to investigate and to serve any organization merely suspected of discrimination with a non-discrimination notice (though often it was only necessary to threaten to issue one) which could be enforced in the courts. These powers were likened by Lord Denning on one occasion to those of the Spanish Inquisition. People who (like the authors of a Fabian tract[3] on the subject which referred to Denning's comment as 'a flight of fancy') are unmoved by these strictures, might take more notice of the comment of Mr Alex Lyon, the former Labour minister. When he was on the Home Affairs Committee which examined the Commission for Racial Equality in 1981, he said that the CRE had been given the strongest powers of enforcement of law against racial discrimination in the Western world and went on to ask what it had done with them. We must ask the same question in relation to the whole period between 1977 and now.

Here is a body which was set up with the duty of increasing racial harmony. It was given substantial resources. Thus in the CRE's first full year, 1978–9, its budget was no less than £4.9 million, rising to £9.4 million in 1985–6. It was required to pursue racial harmony in two main ways. First it was to use its wide-ranging semi-judicial powers, inquisitorial and prosecutorial, though in a conciliatory spirit, to ensure that the law against racial discrimination was obeyed. Second it was to campaign for an end to racial strife and educate the public into dropping its prejudices based on race.

Looking back on a decade of endeavour the Commission for Racial Equality must be considered, to put it mildly, unsuccessful. It can hardly be said to have contributed to racial harmony when the period of its existence has seen the worst race riots in our history. As recently as January 1985, CRE chairman Peter Newsam, surveying the twenty years since the first Race Relations Act was passed, said that racism was getting worse. In support of this contention he mentioned the increasing barracking of black

48

footballers, which had spread from London to Scotland, and the minimal coverage of Britain's black Olympic talent. In his annual report twelve months later he said 1985 would be remembered as a year in which there were serious riots in four inner-city areas. He implied, of course, that it was all the fault of the government, but his own organization, set up specifically to improve race relations, has, far from contributing to that end, been a major part of the problem. In countless instances its efforts have been counter-productive, creating resentment out of all proportion to the 'injustice' it imagines itself to be correcting.

The CRE likes to present its work as so many investigations and cases pursued, so many correctives to racial prejudice adminis-tered, so many promotional exercises to enlighten a benighted public completed. Yet the psychological effect on both the host community and the ethnic minorities has been disastrous. As Andrew Alexander admirably put it,

We have thus now reached the stage where the official and not just the unofficial parts of the race relations industry have one overriding aim: to make us all eat, breathe and sleep 'race' . . . For though the race relations industry may not have succeeded in improving race relations – it has made them vastly more prickly and vastly worse – it has succeeded brilliantly in one thing: making people dead scared of the accusation of being 'racially prejudiced'.[4]

Much of the commission's attention is centred on discrimination in employment. A code of practice which it issued to guide employers would, if followed, require them (or some senior member of the firm who, it is recommended, should be appointed to give attention to matters of race) to spend nearly their whole working day puzzling over whether they have been discriminating unknowingly. For instance, failure to tell the doorkeeper to treat job applicants who arrive at the factory all the same way, might get the management into trouble. Advertisements of vacancies should begin with the ritual declaration that the employer is an equal-opportunity employer and declare no preference for any particular sort of employee. The problem is that almost any job specification could be charged with discriminating against *some* racial minority – in advertising for a tall basketball player, for instance, would one be discriminating against pigmies?

Especially sinister is the covert attempt to oblige employers to accept the idea of racial quotas. Employers are recommended to monitor regularly the ethnic composition of their workforce, not just overall but in 'each plant, department, section, shift and job category and [to monitor] changes in distribution over periods of time'. They are also advised to keep detailed reasons for acceptance and rejection at each stage of the selection process to ensure that no decisions have been influenced by racial factors.

The object of monitoring, it is made clear, is to ensure that ethnics are not 'under-represented', which means not present in the same proportion as they are in the population as a whole (whether district, region, or nation as a whole is not spelt out). Of course there is no earthly reason why the proportion of ethnics in a firm should correspond to that of whatever larger unit of population the lawmakers had in mind. For the qualities demanded of workers are not necessarily distributed evenly throughout society. The guide also gives the impression that monitoring and operating a quota are *expected* of companies; even though no such legal obligation exists. The 'code of conduct' is thus a mixture of deception and intimidation.

Many of the cases the CRE chose to take to court have shown an incredible lack of commonsense. For instance, in 1982 the CRE ruled that the word 'Christian' was impermissible and grounds for legal action when a doctor advertised for a partner who should be a Christian. It later transpired that a dentist had earlier been warned on identical grounds. This was not only offensive but itself indirectly racist, for the ludicrous assumption was that if you were Christian you must be white.

Another complaint lodged by Mr Donald McGrath, a member of the Brent Irish Advisory Service, which the CRE took up and sent to the Attorney General on the grounds that it stirred up racial hatred, concerned a publication called *The Official Irish Joke Book Number 3 – Number 2 to follow*. The sorts of jokes which aroused the CRE's concern were as follows:

What do you call an Irishman with half a brain? – Gifted.

There was the Irishman who tried to gas his wife by throwing her into the North Sea.

Did you hear about the Irish firing squad? They formed a circle.

Sensibly the Attorney General, Sam Silkin, gave his opinion that though the jokes were insulting to the Irish it would be impossible to launch a prosecution. There was no prospect of success in proving that hatred would be stirred up by the book.[5]

A similar case was brought by a Merseyside teacher, who was also race relations officer for the Liverpool National Union of Teachers, against the publishers of *Roy of the Rovers*, the ageless hero of the schoolboy comic strip. It concerned an incident in one of the stories when Melchester Rovers, on tour in the Middle East, had six of their players killed in a terrorist bomb attack. This story was alleged to stir up racial hatred against the Arabs. The outlook of anyone who could spend time and effort on such a farcical prosecution attempt (he even said that if the act was not strong enough to sustain it, it would have to be revised) certainly takes some fathoming.[6]

More important was a case which went to the Appeal Court in July 1982, concerning the refusal of a Birmingham private school to admit a Sikh boy unless he removed his turban and cut his hair.[7] The CRE alleged that this was racial discrimination, though there was no doubt that the school was multi-racial. The Appeal Court, presided over by Lord Denning, decided that a Sikh was not a member of a racial group for the purposes of the act – a blow for commonsense. There was, it decided, no racial discrimination involved, merely a matter of everyone being subject to the same school rules. If the school had been forced to accept the boy then that would have amounted to favouritism. It would have meant that Sikhs were being given a special dispensation to break a rule which everyone else had to keep. That is what Enoch Powell had earlier called 'Communalism' – the giving of privileges to minority groups which are denied to the majority population. Far from improving race relations that kind of thing harms them by suspending the pressures towards conforming with the *mores* of the host community and thus hindering the process of integration. It was extraordinarily perverse of the CRE, but unfortunately quite consistent with many of its other initiatives, to attempt in this way to put up barriers against assimilation, which is where the main hope for harmonious race relations in the future surely lies.

Many have been appalled by the waste of public money involved in the commission's relentless pursuit of hopeless cases. One such was Lord Diplock giving a judgement against the CRE in June 1982. The CRE had gone to the Lords in an attempt to reverse the judgement of the Appeal Court over alleged racial discrimination in Hillingdon. The council of that borough was at its wits' end because it was statutorily obliged to house the homeless who arrived there and, since London Airport was nearby, it bore the full brunt of the large numbers who were arriving by air from abroad. That was bad enough without having the CRE descend on it with additional complaints about its discriminating against some of the immigrants because of their colour, especially when, as Mr Terence Dicks, the council's housing committee chairman, claimed, the CRE's procedures were like those of the 'Star Chamber'.[8]

The high-handedness of many of the CRE's investigations and legal actions was often compounded by the costs which it inflicted on those it had in its sights. In December 1981 Mr Maurice Hulks, chief executive of the Conservative-controlled Slough borough council, wrote to the Minister of State at the Home Office to complain that the commission had abused its powers. A two-year inquiry which it had mounted into Slough's housing policy and abandoned without reaching any conclusion had cost the council £20,000 in legal advice and paperwork. The commission then proposed to institute a second inquiry with slightly different terms of reference but covering much the same ground.[9]

Anger with this sort of behaviour by the CRE found expression in an attempt to introduce a bill for its abolition. It was presented by the Conservative MP Ivor Stanbroke, who described the commission as one of the worst quangos and alleged that it did the opposite of what it was set up to do by emphasizing racial differences and thus promoting discord. He quoted as an example the experience of a London employer who had asked a Job Centre to find him a clerical assistant. There were thirty-two applicants, thirty-one of whom were coloured, and none was found suitable. The CRE then sent the employer thirty-one forms, one for each of the coloured applicants who had not been appointed, demanding to know why not.[10]

Mr Stanbroke's move did not succeed but it was indicative of a widespread and deep-felt irritation with the CRE, which was not only considered incompetent after the 1981 Home Affairs Committee examination of it (which we shall come to shortly), but also to be increasingly authoritarian. This emerged in its bizarre legal contest with the Home Office over its power to investigate immigration procedures.

The CRE had first become concerned with this issue following the widely-publicized 'virginity test' applied to an Indian woman at London Airport in February 1979, as a means of checking whether she had genuinely come to England to marry her fiancé as she claimed. In fact the Home Office maintained that the purpose of the examination was to determine whether the woman had borne children, not whether she was a virgin. Their assumption was that an Indian woman would not have had children outside marriage; if she was found to have had children she must be married already and could not be a fiancée. As a result of the publicity surrounding the test, the Home Office issued instructions that there were to be no more such examinations and arranged for a full enquiry to be made into the use of medical examinations in immigration control.

The matter should have stopped there, but the CRE saw it as an opportunity to raise the question of racial discrimination in immigration control generally. It called on the Home Secretary to institute a public enquiry. When this was not forthcoming it announced its intention to embark on an investigation itself. The Home Office countered with the assertion that immigration was outside the commission's powers because 'Immigration controls do not affect the equality of opportunity of those established here and are not concerned with the interaction of different racial groups.' The matter went to the High Court where Mr Justice Woolf ruled that the commission might conduct the proposed investigation but pointed out that it was not likely to get very far if co-operation by the Home Office was refused.

The chairman of the CRE had already said that the enquiry would not trespass upon immigration policy. As *The Times* commented, the only reason for the Home Office not to co-operate could be that 'it did not trust the commission's discretion or good intentions'. It added that if indeed the Home Office did entertain such doubts 'it must be said frankly that the commission's reputation is not of the highest'.[11] To put the matter a little more bluntly, the commission was obviously making a naked bid for power. It was seeking to wrest control of immigration policy from the politicians and turn it on its head. For whereas all politicians, whatever they had said in opposition, once in power ended up limiting New Commonwealth immigration on the principle all along espoused by Enoch Powell – that assimilation of immigrants was only possible if the numbers were controlled – the CRE was consistently putting forward the diametrically opposite view: that improved race relations would result if immigration policy were more lax.[12] When its investigation was published in 1985 the key recommendation was: 'There should be a major change of emphasis in the operation of the procedures, giving less priority to the prevention of evasion and overriding priority to ensuring that genuine applicants are enabled to exercise their rights with the minimum of delay and difficulty.' This change of emphasis included 'explicit guidance and instruction' to immigration officers that 'inconsistencies in applications arising from efforts to cover up past tax frauds should not delay the issue of entry clearances'.

The CRE's propaganda function has if anything been even more damaging to race relations than its work as an enforcement agency for the 1976 Act. In the latter role it has done harm enough by arousing animosity against the ethnic communities. But, as chief propagandist of the ideology of race equality, it has done even more mischief by fostering a culture of dependency rather than of self-reliance, aggravated by its constant emphasis on minorities' rights rather than their obligations.

This negative approach is especially apparent in a CRE report 'Loading the Law'.[13] It starts by referring to the decisive part racial injustice played in the riots of 1981, implying that they were almost justified because blacks suffered the worst conditions in employment, housing and education for their children. Racial discrimination is then said to compound these disadvantages and to launch blacks on to a 'vicious downward spiral of deprivation'. This portmanteau phrase seems to be an adaptation of the jargon from development economics, the 'vicious circle of poverty' in which many Third World countries are said to be trapped, and it is quite misleading. If the vicious downward spiral of deprivation theory were true, no immigrants would ever prosper, though of course we have only to look at the example of Asians in Britain to see that many of them have done remarkably well.

The report then goes on to advocate in the name of equality of opportunity a programme of bestowing economic privileges on the

54

ethnic minorities (which are all lumped together in the report as 'blacks'). As is common form in such publications it ends with a prophecy which is really more of a threat – that if these changes are not adopted there will be further racial violence. It is fair to ask whether violence has not already been stimulated by such perverse propaganda from an official source.

Further insight into this morbid mentality is given in a CRE research report on 'Employment Prospects for Chinese Youth in Britain'.[14] It paints a picture of a narrow inward-looking community interested only in money-making, traditional to a fault, and with the elders tyrannizing over the young who dare not disobey or disagree. Most young Chinese are seen as exploited by their families who put them to work, usually in the family restaurant. There, it is said, they are given a pittance of an allowance rather than a wage and are trapped with little hope of escape; most of them can't speak English well enough to get jobs elsewhere. The traditional attitude of the Chinese towards education is contemptuously described as: 'simple', being summed up as: 'You'll find wealth and beautiful wives in books, so you must study well.' Many of those who are unemployed do not register for benefits because unemployment is seen as a personal failure and would therefore be a disgrace. 'The Chinese ethnic groups, like many others, regard "signing on" and supplementary benefits as stigmatizing.' Further, although 'there are thousands of catering workers within the Chinese community, there is no union to represent their interests. One of the common beliefs within the Chinese community is that they should look after their own relatives and friends and consequently industrial disputes would be rare and in any event soluble between individual employers and employees.' Jobs are obtained largely through the kinship network, especially in Chinatown. If open disputes arise the workers always lose: even if they are successful at a tribunal all jobs on the kinship network will in future be closed to them. The future of the young Chinese is seen as essentially bleak because they are stuck in the catering trade which is contracting. This view is at least questionable in an age of rapid expansion for the service industries, especially those providing for people's leisure.

The pamphlet concludes with a host of recommendations for government involvement with and assistance for Chinese families, including encouragement of young Chinese to apply for work in which, according to the terms of the 1976 Race Relations Act, they are 'under-represented'. Particularly absurd is the principal recommendation that a multi-cultural curriculum should be introduced in every school, 'so that children can learn and can share each other's culture. This will help them to live in our multi-racial society.' It would be hard to conceive of anything less relevant to the needs of the young Chinese than for them to be initiated in, for example, Afro-Caribbean culture. For, even on the pamphlet's own showing, the biggest drawback the Chinese suffer from in this country is their poor knowledge of English.

It is very revealing that this report should convey the idea that these frugal, hard-working, independent and enterprising people are not to be admired but pitied for not knowing or not caring to know how to claim benefits from the welfare state. For it is qualities such as the sense of purpose and perseverance which the Chinese display that are crucial to economic success. The fact that they reject the dependence which the CRE appears to be urging upon them, and prefer to use their own resources or those of their family or community, suggests that they share the attitudes of their brethren in America, who, despite appalling discrimination, have now clambered into the top income brackets. The notion that the prospects for this community are bleak is the reverse of the truth. It is in fact building up the financial and, far more important, human capital which should make its future affluence secure – as long as it resists the blandishments of the CRE.

It is clear that by its constant harping on the racial aspect of everything under the sun, the CRE, instead of improving relations between the races, has made each one of them more conscious of the ways in which it differs from the rest. Thus instead of helping it hinders the racial integration which is its *raison d'être*. A typical example of this is a report which urged that Urdu should be taught to the English in schools. Indeed Urdu, Bengali, Gujerati, Greek, Italian and the other 125 languages spoken by children in British schools should not be treated as 'foreign', said the report. 'They are not foreign languages,' it insisted, 'but languages of the various communities in the United Kingdom.'[15] A similar approach was found in a CRE publication on bias in the subject matter of school lessons.[16] Classes in cookery which didn't include information on Indian and Chinese cuisine were guilty of racial discrimination, it said. Such a statement is a symptom of chronic cultural relativism –

the theory that all cultures must always rank the same. This is not to deny that other cultures than our own ought to be treated with anything but respect. But our overriding concern must be with the need of immigrant children to acquire as much knowledge as possible of the customs and behaviour of this country, in which their families have chosen to live, and the priority which must be given to understanding English culture cannot be gainsaid.

Of course, good race relations require not only that the racial minorities adapt to the host community's ways, but that members of the host community adapt to the mores of the minorities. This does not mean that they should demean or humiliate themselves, however. Yet how else can one describe the racial awareness courses which the commission is constantly recommending? A report of a seminar on race awareness training[17] published by the CRE argues that the more race-conscious everyone is the better. The abject of a race awareness course is to 'produce in participants a heightened awareness of racism in individuals, including themselves and institutions including their own, reinforced by both fact and feeling, sufficient to ferment a determination to resist and actively to confront racism both personally and institutionally and in the wider society'. With all allowances made for gobbledygook it is clear that the object of the courses is to make everybody more or less race-obsessed. The introductory lecturer maintained that the emotions raised by these courses were guilt and anger at 'those responsible' for racism. Yet, though the responsible ones are, as one might expect, the political establishment, the notion that 'we are all guilty' is also associated with the phrase 'institutional racism'. This abject sense of universal culpability is apparently not to be discouraged but fostered. For, 'Although a racial awareness training course might only last for two or three days, it is important that the participants should meet again as a group, reinforce each other, draw support and plan collective action.' Implanting a sense of guilt is of course a very good way of preparing people for manipulation, and the emphasis on group indoctrination rather than the use of individual judgement has a very sinister ring. It hardly needs saying that the cultivation of heightened race awareness, especially when conjoined with a feverish campaign to denounce manifestations of racial prejudice in any form, is ill-calculated to improve race relations but likely to make them febrile, edgy and unstable.

On other policy matters there is a similar attempt to promote the idea that ethnic minorities must be subject to separate consideration and special rules. A CRE pamphlet on housing need among ethnic minorities,[18] and another on racial equality and social policies in London,[19] both stress the 'racial dimension'. There must not only be a policy for the homeless, but a separate and distinct one for homeless blacks. In local government, Principal Race Relations Advisers directly responsible to the Chief Executive should be appointed and 'many other posts', including 'community workers, teachers, librarians, adult educational outreach workers, housing and environmental health workers and interpreters, all of which posts qualify for S11 funding', filled to ensure that the racial dimension is kept in the forefront of the minds of all who have local power. In the case of London boroughs and the Greater London Council in the Ken Livingstone era this injunction needed no repetition but was put into effect at once. And in a much more recent booklet on the Youth Training Scheme[20] the CRE again condemns the general attitude of *laissez-faire* among the authorities. It urges the appointment of specialists in race relations in every region who should report directly to the top man in each case. Their task would be to push at every point for equal opportunities, and, by keeping ethnic records to ensure that ethnics are not 'under-represented', to introduce racial quotas by stealth.

If, then, as I have argued, the CRE has proved a menace to its own objectives of reducing racial discrimination and promoting racial harmony, is this merely the result of inefficiency? Such seemed to be the message, however diplomatically worded, of the Commons Home Affairs Committee in its 1981 report. It found that the commission's chief defect was 'incoherence'. The commission operated without any obvious sense of priorities or any clearly defined objectives. There were few subjects on which they proved unwilling to pronounce and few projects on which they were unwilling to embark. Yet where specific policy objectives were established they were rarely translated into concrete activity.

Commission staff responded to this policy vacuum by setting their own objectives which, not surprisingly, petered out or went off at half cock. The commission in particular showed a 'lamentable inability . . . to produce completed investigations' – it had started forty-five and completed only ten. The reach of the commission's promotional work was, the committee suspected, beyond its grasp. There was also no proper link-up between investigations and promotional activity. In any case, as the MPs were not alone in thinking, there was some doubt as to whether the two functions of pseudo-judicial enquiry and propaganda were compatible. There were other damning detailed criticisms of the commission's competence, the most notable being its handling of the grants financed by the taxpayer with which it funded 'ethnic minority arts' and even one project aimed at 'joy-spreading'.[21]

All this sloppiness might be put down to poor leadership. In this respect the seeds of the CRE's inadequacy were sown at the very start. For, just as Groucho Marx didn't want to join any club that would have him as a member, so no public figure of real consequence, that is with the stature the post was thought to demand, saw the CRE chairmanship as worthy of him. The job was David Steel's for the asking but he didn't feel impelled to ask, happily as it turned out for the Liberal party. Instead it went to an extremely likeable old Etonian Tory MP, David Lane, who had earlier as a junior Home Office minister had race relations as part of his departmental brief. He had the extra advantage, in the eyes of the Labour government then in power, of being one of the Tory 'wets'. That is to say he had a pronounced belief in the power of government action for good. Shortly after he became chairman-designate, he affirmed his faith in political answers to racial questions by declaring, at a press conference convened to launch a pamphlet, 'Cities in Crisis', for the Tory Reform Group, that central government and local authorities should spend at least £100 million a year to tackle the problem of run-down cities. 'Our second-class citizens of 1976,' he commented, 'are hundreds of inner-city dwellers, white and black, who are trapped by urban deprivation.'[22]

Political heavyweight David Lane was not, but, for the task of CRE boss-man, race relations mouthpiece and friendly neighbour-hood racial watchdog, he had acquired a tone of voice which was to serve him well in the CRE chair until he was blown out of it by the Home Affairs Committee report.

His place was taken in the summer of 1982 by a tough bureaucrat, Peter Newsam, who had a much less cheery personality than David Lane but did seem to have been better at running the office. It is not apparent however that the CRE's impact on race relations improved. Indeed, since it was set up on a false, and indeed perverse, premise – that intolerance can be cured by law – it would be reasonable to assume that the more efficient the CRE becomes the worse race relations will be.

This may seem a paradox at first, but it is by no means unusual in the history of government regulatory agencies – much of it a tale of bodies set up to protect the public being taken over and perverted by the sectional interests they are meant to administer. In the case of the commission, the process has worked more subtly but to the same effect, for the CRE has been largely usurped by the racial minorities it is supposed to protect. Just how far this process had already gone by the time of Peter Newsam's appointment was shown by the fact, which the Home Affairs Committee also pointed out, that 51 per cent of the commission's staff were either black or Asian – hardly their entitlement under a racial quota regime. Such a blatant imbalance has inevitably discredited the CRE and aroused the feelings of hostility it was intended to dissolve. This and other such developments aroused the Home Affairs Committee's alarm and its report was most emphatic:

One aspect of the commission's style has given rise to particular concern. They sometimes seem to adopt the role of spokesman for what they interpret as the views of ethnic minorities, and to prefer this role to their true one of a quasi-judicial statutory commission. The sub-committee therefore sought and obtained from the commission copies of all their press releases for 1980 and the first six months of 1981. Perusal of these confirmed our impression that the commission are at times unduly eager to engage in instant analysis of current political controversy to the detriment of their main statutory duties and at the cost of the reputation for scrupulous impartiality which many of their functions demand.

It did not help that many of the opinion-formers among the ethnic minorities were genuinely under the impression that the commission was intended to be 'their own institution'.

Many of them certainly behaved as it it was. A CRE booklist

about racialism and prejudice in Britain is astonishingly partisan. The books mentioned come largely from bodies like the Runnymede Trust, the Policy Studies Institute and the Institute of Race Relations. They foster the idea that there is a malign conspiracy at work which systematically denies opportunities for ethnic groups to obtain employment, housing, etc. The list makes no pretensions to objectivity and there is no attempt to show that there is another point of view than that of race relations industry personnel.

Again, for a long time the CRE resisted the government proposal in September 1983 to place people who draw the dole into racial groups. Whitehall's object was to provide a picture of the types of people who were unemployed so that government training could help with the right sorts of schemes and language. The CRE's opposition, despite assurances to the contrary, was based on fear that the information might be passed to the Home Office or to immigration officials. The impression given was that the CRE was more on the side of illegal immigrants than of the law.[23]

Another revealing indication of how much the CRE had become identified with the race lobbies was its hostility to the government's proposals in March 1984 for removing from elected local authorities the power to fund ethnic minority groups.[24] This followed the revelation that the Greater London Council had spent £5 million a year to finance minority organizations, and that the ethnic groups among these employed at least 200 community activists. The CRE's warning that, if these people were sacked and sent back to the streets they could provide the focus of future unrest, seemed indicative of the nature of the potentially violent activists. The CRE bias also showed itself in its strong support for the continuation of the Inner London Education Authority, and in many of its interventions during the passage of the 1981 Nationality Act, which restricted British citizenship to those with very close ties with the United Kingdom.

Despite such evidence that the commission has subversive influence within the public domain, Mrs Thatcher's government has resisted attempts to abolish it. The Prime Minister's predominant feeling is probably that abolition would be more trouble than it is worth, especially when there are more important reforms to be carried out. Perhaps the CRE is regarded as a largely innocuous quango which should be tolerated in order to keep the race relations lobby quiet. Such a view is understandable but unwise. Exactly how subversive the CRE is and how unregenerate is its ambition to trample on our tradition of freedom under the law is no longer a matter for speculation. It is published for all to see in the form of proposals for changing the Race Relations Act of 1976.[25] First of all it sets out to widen the scope of the act and of course, as a result, the CRE's own authority. As a preliminary it seeks to ensure that the principle enshrined in the original act, about which many had the gravest misgivings, is enforced without demur. This is that to be found guilty of direct discrimination a racial motive does not have to be proved. It goes on to redefine indirect discrimination to mean 'significant adverse impact'. In practical terms it seeks to impose rather rigid criteria, like a twenty per cent variation from the norm (that is an average share of the community, whatever community is used as marker). Finally it seeks to include religious discrimination within the broad definition of illegal race discrimination.

The plain intention of all this redefinition is to reduce the chances of the commission being overruled in court. With the same aim in view various present exemptions from the application of the act would no longer be preserved. Government services previously outside the act's jurisdiction would be included within it. The Immigration Service, on which the CRE has long cast a covetous eye, would fall within the scope of the act, giving the CRE effective control over immigration policy. It would also extend the act to cover people in occupations over which it had formerly held no sway, such as seamen recruited abroad and people working for airlines. In a very ominous move it demands that, where the act comes into conflict with other laws or statutes, it should prevail.

The business of proving discrimination, over which the CRE has had such problems in the past, would under its own proposals become far easier. The presumption that the CRE's alleged transgressor is at fault would be strengthened by adoption of the principle that the accused is guilty unless he or she can prove the contrary. In other words the CRE would introduce the revolutionary principle into English law that the accused is guilty until proven innocent. Refusal to answer a CRE question would also, it is implied, be considered sufficient grounds for assuming guilt. A further innovation would be to set up a discrimination division within another quango to hear both employment and non-employment race and sex discrimination cases. Legal aid would in addition be available for those pursuing race discrimination cases before these tribunals.

As regards its formal investigations and enforcement of the law relating to race relations, present limits on the CRE's freedom of action would be swept away. The commission would have power 'to conduct a formal investigation for any purpose connected with the carrying out of' its duties. Difficulties experienced by the commission in the ordinary courts would vanish under the new arrangements. Formal notices issued by the commission would not be subject to appeal as at present but would go before an independent tribunal – another quango – for examining the facts of the situation. The commission would be given the right to intervene in any proceedings where discrimination was alleged in order to draw the attention of the tribunal to the likelihood of future discrimination in the situation concerned. In the eyes of the average bystander this must look suspiciously like an attempt to bring pressure for a verdict of guilty.

The tribunal would have power to impose mandatory orders on those found guilty of discrimination. Particularly deserving of attention is the proposal that, in educational cases, powers to prescribe changes in teaching practice would be transferred from the Secretary of State for Education to the tribunal. It is depressing to speculate on how, under such an arrangement, Brent headmistress Mrs Maureen McGoldrick would have fared.

The tribunal would have power to award compensation to those suffering from discrimination, and what a power it would be! For first there would be no statutory limit to the amount and second it could take the form of continuing payments until a stipulated event such as a promotion or offer of employment occurred.

In order to speed up the desired changes the commission would be given power to lay down codes of practice not only for employment but in every other area of economic life. Further, it could prescribe ethnic record-keeping in any public employment and housing with the agreement of the Employment Secretary of State. Finally, where there was under-representation in his workforce, an employer would be entitled to favour the members of any ethnic group.

It requires little reflection to perceive that here is an attempt to

63

introduce a universal system of racial quotas in everything but name. This programme, under the guise of promoting racial equality, would create privileges for racial minorities casuistically justified on the grounds that they would compensate for inequalities which already exist. Although the term is not used it amounts to 'positive discrimination' or, in American parlance, 'affirmative action'. It is objectionable on purely libertarian grounds, as will be considered later. Yet, if necessary to promote the highly desirable objectives of racial harmony and equality, would not the sacrifice be worthwhile? Perhaps the best way to answer that question is to look at the experience of one country, the United States, which has not merely experimented with the idea but applied it on a heroic scale.

5

Lessons from America

If the essence of intelligence is learning from the trials and errors of others instead of from one's own bitter experience, any enquiry into racial problems over here should take account of what has been happening in that great mongrel republic on the other side of the Atlantic, the United States. For though we are apt to think, like General de Gaulle, that the Americans are predominantly Anglo-Saxon, the truth is that there are almost as many US citizens whose ancestors came from Africa as from Britain. Indeed those of British descent are only fourteen per cent of the whole. The feat of absorbing into one nation people of so many and various immigrant races has been a remarkable one by any standards. Yet it was also a racial issue – the slavery of blacks in the southern states – which brought the one serious threat to America's unity in the two centuries since the founding fathers joined together the original thirteen states.

The integration of blacks into America's social, economic and political order has been a mounting preoccupation ever since. It was in the 1960s, though, that the process came to a head in civil rights marches, inner-city riots and the Great Society programme – an attempt, Promethean in its ambition, to expunge poverty and inequality of opportunity, particularly as it affected blacks, from every corner of the nation's life.

Yet if the relevance of the American experience to our racial problems is obvious enough, the actual lessons it has to offer could hardly have been more thoroughly misunderstood, even, or perhaps especially, among acknowledged experts on the subject.

An example of this is Lord Scarman's famous report on the Brixton disorders in 1981. In its conclusion he quoted with enthusiastic approval from an address to the American nation by President Lyndon Johnson in 1968. It was a speech referring to the riots which took place in that year in thirty American cities (which made the Brixton disorders seem trivial in comparison). It went as follows:

> The only genuine long-range solution for what has happened lies in an attack – mounted at every level – upon the conditions that breed despair and violence. All of us know what those conditions are: ignorance, discrimination, slums, poverty, disease, not enough jobs. We should attack these conditions – not because we are frightened by conflict, but because we are fired by conscience. We should attack them because there is simply no other way to achieve a decent and orderly society in America.

Lord Scarman ends with a flourish, 'These words are as true of Britain today as they have been proved by subsequent events to be true of America.'[1]

In fact subsequent events were to show that they were *not* true of America, but at least a part of Lord Scarman's assertion holds up, for they are not true of Britain either. The surprising thing is that, to judge by his bibliography, Lord Scarman appears to have been unaware of the considerable literature of disillusion with the Johnson crusade on behalf of the black poor which had already appeared in America when he produced his report.

One of the early critics to contrast optimistic liberal rhetoric with black lack of progress was Daniel P. Moynihan who, as Assistant Secretary of Labor, had been heavily involved in the Johnson programme. There was also the growing 'Public Choice' school of economists (the leading figure of which, J.M. Buchanan, received the Nobel prize for economics in 1986), which has derided the contemporary idea that governments and their servants are altruists fired by pure benevolence. It is their contention that politicians and bureaucrats are as self-serving as anyone else, in view of which they have constructed a theory of government failure. This is the opposite of the Adam Smith theory of free markets, where each person serving his own enlightened self-interest is guided by an invisible hand to contribute to the good of all. According to the Public Choice doctrine, in the activities of government the pursuit by its servants of their own private purposes (however enlightened) leads through the operations of another invisible hand to unintended and perverse results. These are indeed often the very opposite of those of the policy being pursued.[2]

It is perhaps more remarkable that Lord Scarman should apparently have been unacquainted with the critiques of the Johnson programme from a school of distinguished black American academics. These have various political affiliations but what they have in common is that in their work on poverty they have eschewed wide-ranging indictments of American society and refused to allow the excuse of racial discrimination to become a catch-all explanation applying to every aspect of the plight of the black, especially the urban black, poor.[3] Let us look at the four most important of these academics in turn.

William Julius Wilson is Professor and Chairman of the department of sociology at the University of Chicago. He believes that, as a result of the rapid shift of economic emphasis from the manufacturing to the service sector, success has become increasingly dependent on education. As a result of the famous victories of the civil rights movement over segregation and discrimination in the fifties and sixties, the rewards have increasingly gone to educated blacks. Black college-educated boys and girls have prospered through entering the professions and management. In other words, the black middle class has markedly improved its position. Meanwhile, however, blacks at the bottom of the heap, the black underclass, the unemployed youths, the single black mothers, the unskilled and the welfare recipients, have slid further back. In such a situation, he argues, it is obvious that race matters less than class.

Walter E. Williams, Professor of Economics at George Mason University, Virginia, takes up the same point.[4] He maintains that both blacks and whites, especially the poorer ones, are receiving what amounts to an inadequate education. He supports a voucher system which would allow poor parents to do what the middle classes already do, that is opt out of dud state schools. But what do black leaders say about competition in education? Williams asked the Reverend Jesse Jackson and he replied, 'We shouldn't abandon the public [meaning state] schools.' 'After he said this to me,' says Williams, 'I learned that *he* had abandoned them; he sends *his* children to non-public schools.'

Williams's main theme is that the problems of the black poor are created, not ameliorated, by government. Above all he targets minimum wage laws for the harm they do to poor young blacks. He points out[5] that in earlier times the level of youth unemployment among blacks and whites was the same: by 1976, after minimum wage legislation was passed, black youth unemployment rose to twice that of white youth. This was because employers, being forced to pay a minimum rate, would not take on poorly-qualified workers, among whom there was a disproportionate number of young blacks. Minimum wage laws therefore, though doubtless intended to help the poor black by raising his reward, in practice proved all too often to be the worst kind of race discrimination by pricing him out of a job.

Derrick A. Bell Jnr, Professor of Law at Harvard, is a sharp critic of school integration policies aiming at producing racial balance in schools, and especially of bussing as the method of achieving them. In his view such policies improved neither mutual understanding between the races nor black academic performance. To make things worse the integrationists talked so much, and often quite unfairly, about the inferior quality of education blacks were getting that it made many whites reluctant to send their children to predominantly black state schools.

The most prolific of this new wave of black intellectuals is Thomas Sowell, Senior Fellow of the Hoover Institution, Stanford University.[6] The breadth of his scholarship is astonishing, comprehending not only the experience of America past and present but that of peoples and cultures the world over, and it is difficult in a limited space to do justice to it. He writes not only eloquently but with searing scorn for what he considers the shoddy arguments of America's race relations industry. This animus is fuelled by the anger he feels towards those who he considers have, through their paternalism, which is a kind of inverted racism (for they make the assumption that non-whites are unable to look after themselves) betrayed his fellow blacks. Instead of liberating them such people have fastened on blacks, especially the poorest of them, a new yoke and forfeited their hope of future improvement. For by increasing black dependence on the public purse, their policies have diminished those qualities of personal responsibility and pride in self-reliance through which alone the black underclass can make good their escape from impoverishment to a better life.

Sowell is caustic about the sloppy thinking behind the assertion that where blacks are worse off than the rest of the community in any respect – whether incomes, jobs, housing or education – that this must be due to racial discrimination. For if this were so, how should one account for the fact that the ethnic groups which come out top of almost every American economic league table are the Japanese, the Chinese and the Jews? For all of these groups were until very recently subject to the most severe discrimination through the law, public hostility or vigilante violence.

To those who riposte that the discrepancy is due to colour prejudice, Sowell points out that there are important differences in economic performance among black groups, whose separateness may not be perceptible to outsiders. For instance, second-generation black West Indians there earn on average higher incomes than Americans of German, Italian, Irish, Polish or Anglo-Saxon ancestry. Again, among indigenous American blacks, the descendants of the pre-Civil War 'free persons of colour' are in almost every respect ahead of their brethren who descended from slaves, and have supplied most of the black leadership in America well into the twentieth century.

Of course Sowell does not dispute that there is unfair discrimination against blacks in America, but he doesn't think that it is crucially important – as long as politicians don't interfere. For in a free labour market, for instance, the anti-black employer is likely to find himself paying higher wages for the privilege, as he sees it, of having all-white labour. He may then be undercut by an employer who is without colour prejudice whose labour costs as a result are lower. Thus competition in a free market discourages racial prejudice. Since the artificial barriers were removed against them in American basketball, black players have fully established themselves. In the American music and entertainment industry, which has recently been comparatively free of race prejudice, the Jews and blacks have prospered for the simple reason that impresarios who let bias against the talented people from these groups influence their recruitment of performers would be at a serious competitive disadvantage.

Those who think that political agitation might cure the malady of racism will find little comfort in the writings of Dr Sowell. As he likes to point out, the Japanese and Chinese Americans who have done so well for themselves have kept out of the nation's politics. The Chinese, indeed, have deliberately kept clear of any political entanglement in the South East Asian countries where they have emigrated, despite all the injustices they have suffered, and have concentrated their energies on economic progress. Sowell says that, craven as this may seem in some eyes, it has undoubtedly paid off.

In contrast those ethnic groups which have sought to improve their condition through politics have, comparatively speaking, fared badly. The American Indians, who have had the longest and closest involvement with the American government, have throughout been stuck economically at the bottom of the class. The American Irish, who have also conspicuously engaged in political agitation, have been among the slowest runners of the nineteenth-century European immigrant groups in the prosperity stakes.

In Sowell's view the argument against seeking economic salvation through politics is that it is so unreliable. In America, 'in broad historical terms, government has changed the rules of the game for blacks in virtually every generation'.[7] Nor has it been possible to rely on the consistency of the Supreme Court which since the Second World War has been helpful to black advancement but throughout most of the nineteenth century was, in the eyes of most observers, cast in the role of implacable enemy of the black cause.

Even apparently disinterested political intervention can be harmful to ethnic minority interests. In the last century, US authorities pressed by social reformers tried to regulate conditions of 'sweatshop' workers who, it was thought, were being exploited. Most of them were immigrants and there was a great concentration of them among the poor Jewish immigrants in New York. In fact, says Sowell, the money thus earned was mostly going into savings and creating the financial base which made it possible for the great mass of the Jewish community in the next generation to move out of the slums.

This is not to say that what ultimately matters for getting on in the world is money. What counts far more is human capital, in the form of skills, education, discipline, capacity for work, adaptability, courage, cheerfulness and good health. Some of these, such as good health, are the result of good luck, though good upbringing may play a part. Other qualities which bear on the ability to produce wealth are sometimes the result of a particular ethnic culture, such as the high regard the Jews have for education, which goes back thousands of years, or their knowledge of urban living, which goes back centuries. In America rural Irish immigrants and blacks from the Deep South have taken three generations to adapt to city life.

The notion that governments can, by throwing enough money at 'ignorance, discrimination, slums, poverty [and] disease', foreshorten the period of assimilation of a particular depressed group . is highly doubtful. Politicians who think that they can speed up the process and eliminate differences in economic performance between different ethnic groups by passing laws and making administrative orders requiring affirmative action, not to produce equality of opportunity but equality of result, are set on a dangerous course, as the above criticisms imply. Yet these criticisms, though pertinent, are scattered and diffused and do not convey very specifically just how counter-productive the Lyndon Johnson 'Great Society' programme and its extension under subsequent presidents proved to be. For that we must turn to a remarkable work, *Losing Ground, American Social Policy 1950– 1980* by Charles Murray.[8] It traces the course of the 'generous revolution' which produced a twenty-fold expansion of America's welfare provision, and explains how this enormous undertaking, which only really got going in the mid-sixties, far from achieving its priority aim of eradicating poverty among blacks, left them in most respects worse off than before.

It is saddening nowadays to read the rhetoric which accompanied the launch of the modest Kennedy welfare programme of 1962, with its references to giving the poor 'a hand, not a handout'. The assumption then was that, given the training and the opportunity of a job, able-bodied welfare recipients would swiftly be in a position to look after themselves. Unfortunately the dole queue refused to diminish: in late 1967 a White House presidential aide announced that only one per cent of the 7.3 million people on welfare had acquired sufficient skills and training to make them self-sufficient.

So Johnson announced the next stage of the 'battle for civil rights', that is, 'not just [for] equality as a right and theory but quality as a fact and as a result'. Soon after an executive order required 'affirmative action', meaning deliberate preference in favour of blacks. Let us look at how this new principle performed with regard to poverty, jobs, wages, education, crime and the family.

Poverty

It is generally believed that whatever else the Great Society programme did or did not do it did reduce poverty. In fact there *was* a sharp fall in the numbers below the poverty line, but almost all of it took place before Johnson's programme began. The most telling statistic is for 'latent poverty', that is the number of people who would be poverty-stricken but for government aid. It rose steadily from the late sixties and was unaffected by the seventies boom. This rising population of welfare serfs highlights the failure of the anti-poverty programme because economic independence is crucial to the quality of family life.

Jobs and Wages

From 1965 to 1980 the US federal government spent as much on job-creation as it had spent, in real terms, on the moonshot. Yet this was the very period when black youth unemployment really took off, not only in absolute terms but compared with that of young whites. The figures suggest that young black males especially were flitting in and out of the labour force at the very time when for the sake of their long-term careers they should have been acquiring skills, steady work habits and a good employment record.

The bright side of the picture was that in this period middle-class blacks were breaking through both by obtaining higher-grade jobs (although more than half of them were government posts, doubtless many of them in the anti-poverty programme) and receiving salaries more comparable with whites. Meanwhile, however, the black poor were becoming more than ever stranded in hopeless poverty.

Education

Up until the mid-sixties the education of Americans of all classes was improving. From then until 1980 the gap in educational performance between blacks and whites grew enormously. In 1980 the basic test of recruits' verbal and numerical skills measured by the armed forces showed the white mean score as 2.3 times that of blacks.

Crime

As Murray says, despite their functional illiteracy and lack of skills, young blacks were surviving and one of the ways they were surviving was through crime. Crime rates had been stable until the start of the Great Society programme. It was calculated that, at 1970-levels of homicide, a person living in a large American city had a bigger chance of being murdered than an American soldier in the Second World War of being killed in action. The increase in black arrests for violent crimes during the 1965–80 period was seven times that of whites. Most victims were poor inner-city blacks.

The Family

The original Kennedy welfare plan had as one of its main goals the preservation of the family unit. Yet between the time it was announced and 1980 the black illegitimate birthrate rose from 23 per cent to 48 per cent of the total, while among black teenagers the illegitimacy rate was approaching 100 per cent. Naturally the number of black households with female heads rose sharply. This is important because experience suggests that the members of such households tend to be poor. Indeed the statistics show that in 1980 two-thirds of all poor blacks were living in families headed by a single female.

The popular, as opposed to liberal establishment wisdom in America was that such evidence showed that welfare made people lazy, that soft judges encouraged crime and that there were too many schools devoting their energies to bussing kids instead of teaching them to read. So prevalent did these views become that progressives found it necessary to disprove them. At the Office of Equal Opportunities in Washington they therefore started an experiment involving 8,700 people over a ten-year period, to show that guaranteeing people an income does not turn them into layabouts. In fact it proved, in so far as any social experiment can prove anything, that the assumptions of the federal bureaucrats and their advisers were resoundingly wrong, while completely vindicating the commonsense of the man in the street. Both whites and blacks in the sample did considerably less work while there was a particularly disastrous impact on black family life. The family break-up of the generally poorer Spanish-speaking members of the group was even more calamitous.

It must be emphasized that, in producing this evidence of growing poverty, unemployment, crime, illegitimacy and so on, Murray is not trying to mount a moral indictment of the American blacks. On the contrary he sees them as victims of a policy of 'affirmative' action which, ironically, its proponents regard as the acme of anti-racism. In Murray's and this author's view it is the advocates of the policy who should be indicted. They should be charged with creating, by negligence and wilful refusal to recognize the facts of human nature, a welfare system which promised to make the condition of the black poor better but has instead made it substantially worse.

Murray is saying no more about the American blacks than that they respond to economic incentives like everybody else. The rules were such that young couples were encouraged to live together while remaining unmarried. The rules also encouraged the man not so much to stay in a state of permanent unemployment but to move in and out of the job market. This tendency towards periodic rather than steady employment was especially harmful to the long-term interests of young black males, who were dropping in and out of dead-end jobs and failing to establish either regular work habits or the kind of work record which would help them when they were seeking better, higher-paid jobs later on.

Similarly counter-productive was a rule introduced late in the programme which allowed women to earn $30 without loss of welfare benefit and thereafter to keep two-thirds of any earnings without losing it. Intended to encourage women on welfare to get a job, it actually had the effect of inducing many more working women, who had previously been independent, to go on welfare. This growth in the army of dependants was greeted with perverse delight by many welfare enthusiasts as evidence of how the 'stigma' of being on welfare was being removed, so that people were now claiming federal handouts not as a privilege but as a right.

Those doing less work had more time for crime, but the main reason why the Great Society programme coincided with an explosion of criminal violence and theft is that, for the average murderer, mugger, rapist and robber, deterrents were reduced while incentives increased. From the sixties to the mid-seventies the chances of evildoers being caught, or if caught punished, rapidly declined. In the big cities the judges were strongly influenced by the idea that crime is a response to exploitation and poverty so that deterrence doesn't work. Their compassionate approach to sentencing, especially for crimes by the young, yielded a rich harvest of juvenile delinquency. Meanwhile restrictions on access to court and criminal records of juveniles proved a great boon to youthful offenders.

The same indulgent official attitudes towards misbehaviour in the young in the large urban schools had parallel consequences. Schools which favoured a white middle-class approach towards education and went in for such punishments as suspension and expulsion could soon be brought to heel by being denied federal funds for discriminating on grounds of race. If the school persisted in its old-fashioned ways and tried to maintain academic standards by making students reattempt grades they hadn't passed, the teachers and administrators had to run the gauntlet of court cases brought by pupils or their parents accusing them of infringing their civil rights. Good teachers and good pupils were discouraged while the rebellious and disruptive pupils were let off lightly. No wonder there was a decline in the proportion of schoolchildren who could read, write and count.

Practically all the incentives of the welfare system thus pointed in the same negative direction while each one tended to reinforce the others. As Murray said,

It was easier to get along without a job. It was easier for a man to have a baby without being responsible for it, for a woman to have a baby without having a husband. It was easier to get away with crime. Because it was easier for others to get away with crime it was easier to obtain drugs. Because it was easier to get away with crime it was easier to support a drug habit. Because it was easier to get along without a job it was easier to ignore education. Because it was easier to get along without a job, it was easier to walk away from a job and thereby accumulate a record as an unreliable employee.

It is indeed a case of being trapped in a cycle of deprivation, but not the kind usually attributed by progressives to capitalism. On the contrary it is the ironic result of a public welfare system originally designed to rescue the poor, especially the black poor, from their depressed condition and to give them dignity and independence.

But, says Murray, it was not just a matter of the black poor being given incentives to act against their own long-term interests. The situation was further aggravated by withdrawal of the status rewards for the kind of *positive* behaviour which would enable them to escape to a better life. Once the authorities conceived the view that the poor were not responsible for their condition because 'the system is to blame', then the distinction between the deserving and the undeserving poor disappeared. The poor were all bracketed together as helpless people whose only hope was to be rescued by their betters. Striving and the proud boast of not taking charity from anyone were things of the past, a mug's game when everyone was on the take and welfare an automatic right. Indeed many welfare programmes made failure a condition of eligibility. The old role models, the boys who heroically worked their way up and out of the ghetto through night school and scholarships, were no longer admired but accused of 'acting white', and treated as outcasts or worse.

Murray's book, which has been called the Reagan administration's new bible, concludes that the principles of social action to help the poor must be revised. It is no good treating the laid-off worker in the same way as the drone. It is wrong to put the law-abiding on the same basis as the delinquent. We must be wary of robbing Peter to pay Paul because all transfers tend to be treacherous – what looks like a transfer from rich to poor all too often turns out to be taking from one poor group to give to another. We should handle transfers with the same caution as dangerous drugs – avoid their use unless we are confident that it will add to the world's net happiness: not at all an easy thing to assess.

We had best face the fact that any social reform is of its nature likely to be flawed. If we set up a programme to help poor black criminals, drug addicts, unemployables or illiterates, we at the same time create a demand, and very likely end up offering rewards for being criminals, drug addicts, unemployables or illiterates. A reform which is intended to bring about a change in human behaviour is likely to succeed only if it goes with the grain of human nature. Otherwise it is likely to do more harm than good. The more difficult the problem the more damage it is likely to do.

Judged by these criteria Murray contends that the American social programmes beginning in the last half of the sixties subjected the black poor to new forms of racism worse in their results than the old ones which they were supposed to offset. And he concludes, 'My proposal for dealing with the racial issue in social welfare is to repeal every bit of social legislation and reverse every court decision that in any way requires, recommends or awards differential treatment according to race.'

This is the conclusion of one of America's leading experts about the American Great Society experiment of preferential treatment of racial minorities which has been given the name of 'affirmative action', and which well-intentioned reformers like Lord Scarman and the rather more interested parties associated with the Commission of Racial Equality would have us adopt in Britain.

The conclusion is that, even though it was backed by the resources of the world's biggest and richest democracy, the experiment was a gigantic flop. Not only did it fail to advance the cause and condition of the blacks and the other depressed racial minorities, it actively harmed them. The best thing to do next is to go back to square one.

That is what many Reagan supporters were hoping would happen when he first arrived in the White House. Their disappointment has been eloquently described by David Stockman, the Director of the Office of Management and Budget for four and a half years.[9] He and the other 'supply-siders' were eager to unleash the energies of the American people and through the incentive of tax cuts start a new era of economic growth. But for this to be really effective there had to be corresponding and simultaneous expenditure curbs. Reagan did carry out the largest tax reductions in history but the parallel curtailment of spending never took place. Stockman had singled out the welfare programmes for the largest cuts but their figures obstinately refused to shrink. The Social Insurance and Poverty programme, which absorbed 9.6 per cent of Gross National Product in 1980, was still absorbing 9.5 per cent in 1986. Why did the government falter and the pressure groups succeed?

Stuart M. Butler, Director of Policy Studies at the Heritage Foundation, has recently addressed the question of why conservatives were unable to enlist support for this reform despite the clear failure of the Great Society to eliminate poverty, its primary goal.[10] He claims that first it was because the conservatives did not explain in easily understandable terms why the Great Society welfare state was incapable of erasing poverty. Second, they did not convey a convincing picture of what they would put in its place. Lyndon Johnson's war on poverty, faulty as it proved, at least captured the public imagination.

To start with, let us look at the reasons why the Johnson poverty programme failed so dramatically. First, it was a one-way obligation. The poor were assumed to have an automatic right to welfare but no associated duties. The system was so organized that people were trapped in a state of dependency from which they could not escape.

Second, it was a highly centralized system with, as a result, inflexible rules and standardized assistance packages instead of what was needed – a flexible response to individual needs. This left little scope for local discretion and fresh ideas.

Third, the poor were not able to choose between alternative suppliers of the services they were given. Professional intermediaries such as teachers and social workers chose for them. 'That,' says Butler,

> is why we have public high schools in America where the children cannot read and yet the teachers never have to face competency tests; it is why we have squalid public-housing projects and welfare hotels with prosperous managers; and it is why many adoption services incarcerate children in institutions, drawing thousands of dollars a year in management fees, rather than place a child with a family and lose their government grant.

From this diagnosis emerges an alternative vision of welfare. Instead of a 'free-lunch system' there would be a '*workfare system*'. Rather than being simply entitled to government handouts their recipients would either train or perform whatever work they can. Individuals would have to take responsibility for their dependants. If a teenage boy fathers a child he should be obliged to support it through his job or public sector work; if he refuses he should be jailed.

Again, parents should be responsible for the actions of their children, as in the state of Wisconsin. There the parents of any teenager who becomes a parent must contribute towards any welfare assistance provided by the state. Priority concern for the innocent child should mean that welfare payments do not encourage unmarried teenage mothers to get up an 'independent' household where she and the child are condemned to a lifetime of unemployment and welfare dependency. In short the aim is to strengthen by all possible means the principle of self-help.

Next, welfare must be decentralized from the government to what Glenn C. Loury, professor of political economy at Harvard, calls 'mediating structures'[11] which stand between the individual and public authority, such as the family, church associations and other private bodies. The traditional family's role as the bulwark against poverty should be encouraged, especially since the scourge of child poverty is concentrated in families with one parent not two.

As far as possible neighbourhood welfare arrangements should take the place of national welfare arrangements. Everyone has a structure of loyalties, with the family normally coming first, then the local community, extending outward in a series of widening and weakening circles to the nation. The closer, more immediate and more familiar the influence, the stronger and more sympathetic the bond. By experimenting with schemes involving different combinations of these loyalties, welfare should not only be decentralized but diversified.

Finally, the stranglehold of the professional service suppliers must be broken by giving the power of choice to the welfare poor. Instead of the teachers having control of the children's education, vouchers should transfer it to parent power. Similarly, efficient, convenient and economical public housing is found where tenants take over the management themselves.

A welfare system on these lines would reinforce the social structure instead of destroying it as the present one has tended to do. Stuart Butler is harking back to Churchill's commonsensical attitude to welfare – that it should be a springboard, not a featherbed. It is an approach which, if applied to Britain's welfare services, could, from the ethnic minorities' point of view, have admirable results.

6
Race and Riot

Britain in the 1980s has been the scene of race-related riots and urban disorder unprecedented in modern times. For the British public the spectacle, made vivid by TV, of ferocious mobs of largely black youths, not in just one but several cities, engaging in pitched battles with the police was traumatic indeed. For a people grown complacent in the assumption that this sort of thing only happened abroad, it was shattering. The knowledge that, in these conflicts, hundreds of policemen were injured and that in 1985 in the Tottenham riots on the Broadwater Farm Estate Police Constable Blakelock was murdered, generated countrywide alarm.

One might have expected these events to have been the occasion for self-satisfied pronouncements of the 'I told you so' variety from those who had previously condemned our lax immigration policies. Yet Enoch Powell and others were perhaps content to let these awful events speak for themselves. It might also have been appropriate if the race relations industry had reacted at least with a modicum of restraint. Some confession of their own part in the failure by those who were paid to foster race harmony might not have come amiss. Yet if such penitence was there its profile was not very high. The race relations professionals we did hear from bore a different message altogether. Far from taking some responsibility for the disaster upon themselves they rose up and denounced British society with even greater vehemence than before. For them these disorders were the condign rewards of

81

endemic racism among the white majority. And, if the original natives of these islands stood accused, so in even greater measure did those who were officially deputed to act on their behalf. The police were portrayed not as law and order's front line of defence but as white supremacists, agents of oppression and exponents of brutal tactics intended to provoke.

Yet more culpable in the eyes of the race relations establishment were the politicians, particularly of the Thatcherite government, which in its view had pursued ethnically discriminatory policies over employment and housing that unavoidably created or exacerbated the deprivation and despair against which rioting and mob violence were legitimate forms of protest. Anyone who believes this statement of the view of the race relations lobby is unfair should consult the opening paragraphs of the 1985 Annual Report of the Commission for Racial Equality, of which it is little more than a summary. Indeed the tone of the report was rather more abrasive: 'Most of those directly involved, in many cases as victims, were black. Most of those involved in suppressing the riots, in commenting on them or simply watching them on their television screens, were white.'[1] Note the suggestion that blacks were 'victims' even though they were the people doing the rioting and as if there were no victims among the police. Note too the implication that the white majority was somehow at fault purely on the grounds that they were watching the riots on television. For it is hardly remarkable that the commentators were largely white; they would have to be, given their weight in the total population, even on a quota basis. Only people who are paranoid about race could lump together facts of this kind and read racist oppression into them. Rarely has the widespread suspicion that those whose profession it is to combat racial conflict have a vested interest in promoting it been more convincingly displayed.

The real danger of such an approach, however, lay not in its expression by bureaucrats of the race relations industry but in its adoption by a British law lord in an official report on the Brixton riots. The moderate tone and judicious language of Lord Scarman should not deceive anyone into believing that his report was impartial. Predictably it has become the bible of the race relations lobby, providing a fund of authoritative-sounding quotations to justify all manner and variety of mischievous and costly public intervention. The Church of England also followed in Lord

Scarman's wake. Its Whitehall-style report, 'Faith in the City', was important not in itself but for its indication of how pervasive the doctrines of anti-racism have become among the politically articulate. Here I shall take what I hope is a fresh look at the facts of race-associated violence and try to expose the fallacies which the race relations industry and others have put forward in presenting their diagnoses and cures.

Initially the interpretation of these events was left to the 'liberal' intellectual establishment and the race relations industry which forms part of it. Here I use the adjective 'liberal' in the American sense, which is in effect equivalent to 'socialist'. Even so I stick to the word because it is a label in common use in the West and has a broad appeal which 'socialist' lacks. 'Liberal' still evokes a generally friendly response because it retains the cachet of the old values, despite the fact that in its present incarnation they have been inverted. It was once a title proudly assumed by individual-ists. As a philosophy of government it awarded moral prizes to those who shouldered personal responsibility for their actions and believed that progress was furthered by maximizing the indi-vidual's freedom under the rule of law to pursue his or her own personal goals. It was not, as it has since been misrepresented, a gospel of selfishness; as the spectacular growth of Victorian charity showed, it incorporated the notion of 'caring', which was given practical expression by people who voluntarily contributed their money to charitable causes.

By a curious sleight of hand this idea of liberalism, the vintage Gladstonian variety which made the individual the centre of the moral universe, has been turned upside down. The concept was collectivized partly by the Fabian socialists and partly by an extremely influential Oxford don, T.H. Green, who in turn reflected the collectivist leanings of the intellectually fashionable German idealist philosophers of the time. According to their scheme of things, if one individual was impoverished then that was a blemish on the common good. For this we were all guilty and therefore collectively responsible for remedying the wrong. That this notion has found its way into the race issue shows how far the old and noble philosophy of personal responsibility has been perverted. Individual racist acts are condemned but regarded as understandable to the point of being almost excusable since they reflect society's institutionalized racism which cannot, it is argued, be remedied except by collective action, that is by the initiative of politicians using the agencies of the state.

This was the knee-jerk response of the Labour party to the Brixton disorders, which took place within a short bus-ride from the House of Commons. In an emergency debate on the subject Michael Foot, the then leader of the Labour opposition, put the blame squarely on government economic policies for causing 'the greatest increase in youth unemployment that the country has known'. This, though an orthodox socialist pronouncement, found sympathetic echoes among members of the Tory party generally referred to as the 'wets', some of whom were even sitting, if rather uncomfortably, on the government benches. Among their number was Willie (now Lord) Whitelaw, the Home Secretary. An interpretation in Fleet Street at the time was that Whitelaw and others (notably James Prior, the Secretary of State for Employment), saw the riots as an exposure of the flaws in Thatcherism and as an opportunity to reinstate the 'Butskellite' consensus economic policies which they preferred and which had prevailed before Mrs Thatcher came to office. Perhaps so, but it is more likely that Whitelaw invited the eminent Lord Scarman to prepare an official report principally in order to buy time. For Whitelaw had always been less of an ideologist than a parliamentary tactician. Setting up an enquiry was for him a way of pigeon-holing a problem which could do his government no good.

In the first instance Scarman's remit was to enquire into the inadequacies of policing which had led to the riots in Brixton (later widened to include the disturbances in Southall, Toxteth and Moss Side and the West Midlands). The noble lord then requested that his terms of reference should be broadened to include the social and economic causes as well. It is no reflection on his integrity but a recognition of his general cast of mind to say that the broad shape of Lord Scarman's conclusions was predictable from the word go. His investigation, naturally, required him to demand evidence from all the interested parties. The marker for the race relations lobby was put down by the Commission for Racial Equality. Its evidence, its main line of reasoning and many of its demands, though not its hectoring tone, provide much of the stuff of the eventual report.

The CRE's submission was indeed a disagreeably complacent document, developing the 'You should have listened to us before' theme and making copious use of its own previous publications, a little more attention to which, it claimed, would have enabled the authorities to nip the riots in the bud. 'A disregard of previous reports and recommendations,' it says, 'was a significant contributory factor in Brixton.' An unfortunate reference came near the end of the submission in what was clearly intended to be a withering attack on the failure of the authorities to learn from the earlier social disorders in American cities. It cited the refusal to take on board or to benefit from the work of the Kerner Commission, set up to investigate the causes of America's riots in 1968. According to John O'Sullivan, a former *Daily Telegraph* staffer by then editing a Republican political quarterly, *Policy Review*, in Washington, the citation of Kerner as an authority on civil disorders was the source of amazement among newspapers over there. For the report was as discredited as its author, Otto Kerner, who was later convicted of bribery, income tax evasion, perjury, conspiracy and mail fraud. The Kerner Report had concluded that the riots were caused by 'white racism', black poverty and powerlessness. It also arrived at the sensational conclusion that the black rioter was, in O'Sullivan's words 'a most superior person, better-educated and more politically committed than the dull and self-effacing non-rioter'.[2] Yet in fact, as O'Sullivan pointed out, both these conclusions had been shot down. Kerner had not been able to show any causal link between the riots and black grievances. The riots had occurred in parts of America where blacks were relatively well treated. The studies of both arrested and non-arrested rioters showed that the rioters had no more grievances than the others and both groups felt that they had made substantial economic progress. As for the alleged superior education of those who had rioted, this was apparently based on a statistical error.

Of course it is not surprising that the CRE should have been beguiled by the Kerner Report or tried to market its 'lessons', since these tune in so harmoniously with its own views. These views were (and are) much as one would expect of a mouthpiece of the ethnic minorities, which, as has been pointed out earlier, is what the CRE has become. Of course the CRE will deny this, but it is surely evident in the fact that, apart from one introductory comment to the effect that police/community relations are a two-way street, the whole emphasis of its submission to Scarman was on what public bodies could do for blacks, with scarce a mention of what blacks could themselves contribute to improved race relations. Indeed, in the list of recommendations, there was no suggestion that the black minority had any duties at all.

Another example of the blinkered character of the CRE's submission was its attempt to whitewash (if such a word may be used without infringing the CRE's code of conduct) the Lambeth borough council, which indeed it congratulated for 'its invaluable work for racial equality'. The Lambeth council's behaviour on a whole range of matters has been so reprehensible that it doubtless needs all the praise it can get, but the CRE's eulogy was absurd. The 'Report of the Working Party on Community/Police Relations in Lambeth' issued under its auspices and with its enthusiastic approval was a disgracefully unbalanced piece of work. It described the police force in the borough as 'an army of occupation' and referred to operations by the Special Patrol Group as 'attacks by the SPG on the people'. Again it reported, 'Our evidence on beat police suggests that they are a liberal façade for the increasingly centrally controlled militarization of the police.' Scarman, who was fairly indulgent towards most of the groups coming to him, was in this instance visibly frosty. He had no doubt that, though it reflected attitudes prevalent in the borough since 1979, the Lambeth working party's report had succeeded in worsening relations with the police.[3]

The 'invaluable work' that the CRE attributed to the Lambeth borough council presumably referred to its employment of a large contingent of race relations bureaucrats in housing, social services and management services and its numerous measures of positive discrimination in favour of ethnic groups, of which the CRE so strongly approves, including a special programme to promote these groups and inform individuals of their rights.

A more critical approach might have made the authors pause to consider why it was that the worst riots should break out where the race relations cohorts had been at their most active. It would have at least considered the possibility that so much activism was counter-productive.

The CRE submission also attempted in an ingenious diversion to deflect the criticism that the Lambeth working party was extremist (its extremism was the reason the police gave for refusing to participate in it). It said, 'Phase 1 of the Inquiry will assess how far political extremists may have helped to provoke the disorder (and the National Front offices now established in Streatham must not be overlooked).' Needless to say those who were complaining about political extremists were not thinking of the activities of the National Front but of left-wing agitators in the working party itself. It went on, 'Even if evidence of extremist provocation should be found, to attribute all the expressed grievances of Brixton to political agitation would both exaggerate its impact and obscure the real processes by which resentment builds up in a community – through the experiences of ordinary people passed on to their families and friends.' But this was to prejudge an important question without offering any evidence at all. The truth is that the CRE couldn't bring itself to contemplate the possibility that extremists were a factor in causing the riot because this would contradict the version of events it had every interest in promoting.

As for the CRE's recommendations, they consisted of a whole range of proposals for removing racial disadvantage, which predictably amounted to the conferring of special privileges on ethnic minorities – the nostrums they had been peddling for years. In the important opening section concerning what central government should do, the CRE called for changes in the law to give the ethnics greater protection, monitoring of racial disadvantage (implying a policy of covert racial quotas), more government money and administrative action to support ethnic 'needs' in respect of employment, housing, training and business loans. Other recommendations followed covering yet more areas of policy, demanding that blacks be given further rights and financial assistance. More significant was the section dealing with the police, for out of nine proposals in this section Scarman adopted six. These were:

Improved community policing techniques.

Screening out of racially prejudiced police recruits.

Racism-awareness training sessions for the police.

More and more effective community liaison staff to be employed.

Direct and constant dialogue between the police and members of the black community.

In pointing this out I am not trying to suggest that Lord Scarman was a pushover for the CRE. The more likely explanation is that the CRE, which had been developing programmes of self-aggrandizement for years, was ready and waiting when the call for changes came following the Brixton troubles. To some this might appear to be democracy at work, but it is more to the point to see it as the classic process by which quangos grow. The CRE, as we have seen, was the last of a series of race relations bodies appointed by central government to smooth out race relations at times when they were getting rough, and also to demonstrate that the government of the time was 'doing something' about the politically contentious matter of race. It was soon hijacked by the ethnic minorities it was supposed magisterially and benevolently to oversee, and has consistently sought to magnify its own authority and extend the power of those who claim to give racial minorities a lead. When a crisis occurs in a racially mixed area, CRE pooh-bahs are inevitably appointed expert witnesses before another quango – a judicial enquiry; for this second, short-lived quango is established principally to damp down passions and can hardly help taking seriously the 'specialists' from the semi-governmental body intended to supervise race relations. The 'specialists'' evidence therefore has a great influence on the final report. Later the police come under pressure to show they are responding to its recommendations. The result of this is that, in effect, those who have been attacking the police end up having a big say in their reform.

In this particular instance the process went much further and the race relations lobby extended its influence more widely. The Scarman Report has itself exerted a profound influence on the content and form of public argument over race and disorder ever since. By its conclusion that the conflict was 'neither premeditated nor planned' but 'erupted from the spontaneous reaction of crowds to what they believed to be police harassment', prime responsibility for the riot was removed from the rioters. Although the report did refer to a 'sinister contribution' of strangers rioting and distributing petrol bombs, this was mentioned only to be dismissed. For all its qualifications, and the Scarman Report contains a great many, the blame in the end falls first on the police, against whom there was 'an outburst of anger and resentment by young black people', and second on underlying social conditions. It followed that, if the police were at least partly to blame, it was necessary for them to reform their ways. That called for new policies in police recruitment, training, methods, monitoring and discipline. It should be understood throughout the force, said the report, that the normal penalty for racially prejudiced behaviour is dismissal. Policing in the racially mixed inner cities should be 'sensitive'. Scarman was particularly critical of such 'insensitive' operations as 'saturation' policing, stop-and-search operations and (the use of) units like the Special Patrol Group. There should be an independent complaints procedure and, though Scarman rejected local authority control of the police, obligatory consultation with local authorities on a continuous basis.

While very properly insisting that the law should be the same for everyone, Scarman's recommendations essentially amounted to the police pursuing a softly-softly policy in racially sensitive areas. Well might the average Bobby on the beat be bemused by Scarman's abjuration to be not merely 'firm' about applying the law but 'imaginative' as well.

Yet, important as this 'reform' of the police has been, the main thrust of the Scarman Report was straightforwardly political. Ultimately the noble lord was far less concerned about police misconduct than about the political attitudes which determined the 'underlying conditions' of the ethnic groups. He plainly did not expect the necessary changes to be brought about by any efforts by members of the ethnic community themselves. The report finally translated into a call for intervention by a paternalist state. The prescription was based on Lord Scarman's observation that Brixton, with its black population of 36 per cent, suffered in extreme form from the social problems and general deprivation common to inner-city areas. These were:

Severe housing problems and lack of adequate leisure and recreational facilities.

Family problems, with a high proportion of one-parent households. (The majority of children in care in the wards where the riots took place were black.)

Under-achievement by many West Indian children in Brixton and failure to acquire the language, culture and skills needed to obtain employment, despite much dedicated work in the schools.

The higher and also longer lasting unemployment of blacks in the area to a great extent caused by employers' discrimination.

While Lord Scarman did not excuse young blacks of Brixton from responsibility to uphold public order he did not, to judge from this litany of their misfortunes, appear to believe that they had much responsibility for their 'underlying conditions'. The implication of his diagnosis was that only the authorities could materially improve their position. His report was indeed an indictment of the alleged injustice and inefficiency of Britain's law enforcement regime and of the public social provisions for racial minorities, with political action offering the only means through which these defects could be redeemed. It was the judgement of a powerful mind which nevertheless, despite appearances, ignored more than it illuminated.

Scarman's main conclusion, that the Brixton riot was spontaneous, is open to doubt. BBC Television was warned of the riot by a phone call two hours in advance. Large groups of black youths were forming beforehand while various whites with cameras were photographing every move the police made. A number of left-wing agitators were recognized in the mob. Some helped to make Molotov cocktails, which, together with iron bars, were available in suspiciously large quantities.[4] These facts suggest that, far from erupting spontaneously, the riot was planned in advance by people who were manipulating Brixton's black youth in an attempt to destabilize this country's democratic society.

As regards the conduct of the police, on Scarman's own showing one of their main failures in Brixton was not to quell the riot as soon as it began. At least in this respect the policing at the time of the disturbances was not excessively harsh but not harsh enough. In fairness it should be said that Scarman's strictures were levelled against the saturation policing of the area prior to the outbreak in the so-called 'Operation Swamp', which amounted to provocation. Yet this operation was mounted in response to keen local concern over the high level of muggings and other street crimes. The alternative was for the police to accept in practice that, where communities are hostile, no-go areas are an inevitable fact of life. It was all very well for Lord Scarman to deny this and to argue that the real alternative was and is greater police/community co-operation. For where such co-operation did not spontaneously occur, as in the borough of Lambeth, the police, if they had simply allowed the street gangs to carry on mugging, would have failed in their primary task. As a result of Scarman's report, however, the attitude of the authorities towards black law-breakers became less firm.

Nor was the situation improved by the broken-backed way in which the law finally dealt with the culprits. Although 292 Brixton rioters were arrested, a month later only a third had been processed by the courts and not one of the arrested had been sent to gaol.[5] One phrase in the Scarman Report which lingers in the mind occurs in his description of young rioters who 'found a ferocious delight in their activities'. This parallels what was remarked upon by Professor Banfield of Harvard University in his book *The Heavenly City* in a chapter entitled 'Rioting Mainly for Fun and Profit'. There he argued that riots, instead of expressing some general resentment or sense of political injustice, were only examples of 'animal spirits and of stealing by slum-dwellers, mostly boys and young men'. A potent factor in their behaviour, he argued, was the realization that they had little to fear from the police and the courts. Police, under threat from civil rights legislation if they put a foot wrong, tended to look the other way when blacks committed crimes. The courts, influenced by progressive sociologists, tended increasingly not to enforce the law against offenders who were young, poor and black.

John O'Sullivan's article, already referred to,[6] also cites the analysis of Miss Midge Decter in a feature in the American magazine *Commentary*, about the New York looting.[7] She said that their elders and betters in the liberal establishment had been telling young blacks for years in newspapers, magazines, TV and radio 'that they are inherently and by virtue of their race inferior. They must not be judged by the standards which apply to everyone else . . . It is, to be blunt about it, the message of liberal racism.' As for the idea that stopping a riot by using enough force to crush it is mere tinkering with the problem and that it is necessary to deal with the underlying social causes, O'Sullivan quotes the riposte of

Professor Van Den Haag: 'This view suggests a fireman who declines fire-extinguishing apparatus by pointing out that "in the long run only the elimination of the causes of fire can make a significant and lasting difference . . ." Firemen who behaved like this would, rightly, be accused of passing the buck.' Talk of underlying causes is no excuse. Some causes of conflict are hundreds of years old – like the Catholic versus Protestant enmity in Ulster, the Walloon versus Fleming struggle in Belgium, or the clash between French- and English-speaking people in Quebec. The solution of these stubborn problems is not something we can afford to argue about while failing to suppress the violence they cause.

In a brilliantly perceptive article the *Economist* also scorned the idea that the Brixton troubles derived from a sudden explosion of black wrath. It doubted whether there was any generalized cause for riots: '. . . hooligan disorders periodically break out in summer in most big world cities. . . . A particular law or careless act of policing upsets the normal pattern of local order and triggers violence.' It pointed out that ever since the Notting Hill riots in 1958, parts of most British cities have seen periodic outbursts of aggression usually against the police and selected properties (mostly derelict or abandoned). It claimed that there was no central motivation in the Brixton riots apart from young blacks being angered by what they considered to be discriminatory policing. Disorders spread because whites as well as blacks saw on television how easy it was to get away with looting.

If the riots had really been protests against unemployment, why had they not appeared in Glasgow and Tyneside where the level of unemployment is among the country's highest and most pro-longed? Nor is it necessary to be unemployed in order to riot, as white British football fans have demonstrated all over Europe. The worst riots of the seventies were among blacks whose unemployment level was lower than that of blacks elsewhere in Britain who were quiescent. Again, if the riots were really a protest against lack of government support for deprived areas, why did they break out in Toxteth, which had received more government financial help over the previous decade than almost any other district in Britain?[8]

The reaction to the Brixton riots was thus an extreme example of falsely attributing local events to cosmic causes and particular problems to general grievances. At the time Andrew Alexander in the *Daily Mail* attacked attempts to explain the Brixton riots as the result of the number of blacks out of work.[9] Why, he asked, if the length of the dole queues determined the degree of disorder was Northern Ireland, where they were longer than anywhere else, at the time comparatively peaceful? As he went on to add, when the Ulster troubles had been at their height, the British press produced a quite different set of explanations for the unrest. Then it was said that the marchers were angry about denial of civil rights, or, more specifically, unfairness in the allocation of council houses and limitations on the franchise in council elections. Yet when the Protestant ascendancy was ended and these injustices removed, the troubles did not end any more than, Alexander predicted, the disturbances in Brixton would cease when unemployment was reduced. His belief was that the root of the trouble in both Ireland and Brixton lay in people who wanted to undermine the political system. They knew that if marchers came into conflict with the police this could prompt a reaction which some would dub 'police brutality'. Official enquiries could then be demanded and acceded to which by criticizing the police might reduce police morale, thus taking the opponents of our political system closer to their ultimate objective of overthrowing it. Undoubtedly this is another generalized explanation but it is more convincing than Scarman's determinism, according to which, given bad social and economic conditions, riots inevitably erupt.

There is little doubt that the police sought in good faith to carry out the bulk of the recommendations of the Scarman Report regarding recruitment, training, community liaison and consultation in a genuine attempt to diminish racial animosity against them. Nor was this policy a flash in the pan in the immediate aftermath of the riots. The political pressure to expunge racism from the police was maintained after the departure of Whitelaw to the Lords and the arrival at the Home Office of Leon Brittan. In May 1984, for instance, Brittan issued a directive to the Metropolitan Police Commissioner and the forty-two chief constables of England and Wales to keep records of all officers disciplined for all matters involving racism. This policy had in fact already been started the previous January following a critical report by the Policy Studies Institute[10] which had been ordered by the Metropolitan Police Commissioner at the time, Sir David McNee, just before he retired. It found, after three years' study, that the police force was deeply infiltrated by racial prejudice and racist talk. To the enquirers one source of 'serious concern' was that young men of West Indian origin had the highest chance of being stopped by the police. Yet if the chances of their being stopped by the police were the same as those of the rest of the population there would have been cause for more serious concern, for crime rates for West Indians were, in proportion to their numbers, very high indeed. This fact was clear from figures issued by Scotland Yard in March 1983 which showed that, in the previous year, of 19,258 muggings reported in London, 10,960 were committed by blacks.

Of course it is true that the identification of muggers as black may not always be accurate as many of the muggings take place in the dark. The evidence, however, of a research report in September 1984 which investigated the number of black prisoners in British gaols was not open to this criticism as their colour could be verified by daylight. What it showed was that, in the south east of England, whereas young whites outnumber young blacks by thirty to one in the population as a whole, in youth custody centres the ratio was only three to one. The term 'blacks' was not used in the report in order to distinguish between West Indians and Asians, who are often lumped into this general category. In fact, though in the population as a whole Asians numbered one in twenty, in the prisons they were one in seventy, that is they were far less prone to crime (or at least to going to prison for it) than the rest of the nation.[11] This undeniable evidence does show that there is a hugely disproportionate number of blacks sentenced for crimes, and the clear implication is that they commit more crimes.

The disproportionate amount of crime committed by West Indians would account for another conclusion of the report, perhaps disturbing at first sight, namely that the West Indians have substantially more than average contact with the police as offenders and suspects. Nevertheless the police took the report's conclusion seriously and sought ways of reducing racial prejudice in the force. That positive results could be achieved was shown in the matter of racial attacks. The House of Commons Home Affairs Committee criticized the low clear-up rate of this crime – only 13 per cent in 1984 and 15 per cent in 1985 – in the Metropolitan area compared with 64 per cent in Avon and Somerset. Yet in one Metropolitan borough, Tower Hamlets, the record palpably improved. There the police had local training, put more constables on the beat, had a twenty-four-hour helpline, used local volunteers from the Bangladeshi community, established a multi-agency forum for discussing cases and gained local confidence with a commitment to firm action. As a result the clear-up rate rose from 8 per cent in 1984 to 31 per cent in 1985.[12]

As well as attempting to induce the police to follow the recommendations of the Scarman Report, the government also accepted an amendment to its Criminal Justice Bill from peers led by Lord Scarman to make racial discrimination by police officers a criminal offence. His Lordship had urged the change, saying that no single step could be more effective in building up black people's confidence in the police.[13]

A strongly contrasting view was put by Sir Eldon Griffiths, a Tory MP and parliamentary adviser to the Police Federation, who gave a friendly but serious warning about police morale. 'I have not known a time,' he said, 'when the police have felt so let down by their friends,' and added that they had been 'astounded' that the government should lend its authority to such an amendment when they were under attack from stones and petrol bombs and from the rear in Labour-controlled authorities.[14] He further remarked in an article in the *Daily Express* that while Parliament was debating the Police and Criminal Evidence Act, the Greater London Council spent more than a million pounds on publicity which portrayed the police as racist oppressors. In support of this contention he referred to a pamphlet issued by certain GLC-financed women's organizations which suggested that white doctors, backed by the police, would use contraceptive jabs available through the National Health Service to 'solve the immigrant problem' by rendering black females infertile. He summed the position up as follows: 'A powerful combination of the civil liberties and race relations industries, local politicians, pundits and the know-it-alls of TV have been guaranteed to hold the police – not the rampaging youths – responsible for racial clashes.'[15]

The government and the police authorities thus made a real and sustained attempt to reduce all manifestations of racism in the force. Whether these urgings always had the desired effect on the constabulary is more open to doubt. To the man on the beat the race issue was one more complication in a task which was difficult enough in a period of rising crime. Monitoring racism, like monitoring anything else, meant more form-filling and bureaucracy. There was bound to be resentment among the rank and file at the extra burden and at the constant need, where ethnic suspects were concerned, to watch their step. One small grievance was a report that the police in Brixton should not, while on duty, wear a tie commemorating recent riot operations in the borough as it was thought to be in bad taste and likely to provoke ill-feeling. More ominous were the words of the Metropolitan Police Commissioner, Sir Kenneth Newman, following a visit to the 'front line' in Brixton soon after his appointment. In a solemn and considered statement he said: 'They are being spat upon. They are being gratuitously abused. They are having things thrown at them for no reason at all. And there are attempts to trap them into ambushes.'[16] This came from an officer who was as committed to 'sensitive' policing in multi-racial areas as anyone and who, having just come from service in Ulster, knew a thing or two about riots. He recognized the danger-signals of a situation where the police were showing all the 'sensitivity' while, from the population it was protecting, indifference or sullen hostility was the only response.

Certainly there was no let-up in the activities of the Greater London Council's Police Committee, chaired by Paul Boateng, who was notoriously hostile to the police. The GLC put aside £400,000 to set up and service independent police monitoring groups whose purpose seemed to be nothing other than discrediting the capital's police force. One of these groups, established in Croydon, was reported to be run by twenty-eight-year-old Femi Adelaja, a postgraduate student in physics, who told a reporter: 'Black people in Croydon and Brixton and many other areas in London . . . hate the Metropolitan Police.' He conceived his job to be to 'protect the people, not to cause race riots or conflicts'. His method, however, was to organize what were in effect vigilante groups of four men carrying walkie-talkies. He went on to enthuse, 'We know from experience that we can get 200 of our people on to the street within minutes and hundreds more if necessary within a very short time.' Local Asians complained that the effect of these arrangements was that if one of them got into a dispute with a West Indian, 'before we know what's happening we're surrounded by blacks'. Needless to say such big buildups of crowds of black youths, especially where police were present, could easily be the prelude to a riot. The real purpose of this monitoring seems indeed to have been protection of a more sinister character. As Adelaja put it himself, 'We're going to do a Special Branch on the Special Branch. We'll soon have a file on every London policeman and their racial attitudes.'

Would that Mr Adelaja could have been shrugged off as some kind of fanatic. Alas, his postures are all too typical of the left in Inner London wherever they are able to wield power. For instance there was the anti-police bias injected into school examinations. This is what Stuart Sutton, political adviser to the then Secretary of State for Education, Sir Keith Joseph, was complaining about in June 1984. He said that a Whitehall-backed report showed that at Tulse Hill Comprehensive in South London teenagers were given exam questions portraying the police as racist and the traditional family as out of date. One question read: 'Describe the harassment many black people have faced as a result of immigration controls in two of the following areas: police raids, detention centres, family break-up, hospital treatment.' Another question in the 1982 CSE paper asked pupils to comment on how the West's multi-national companies have harmed the interests of Third World people.[17] Again, the Inner London Teachers' Association, representing all members of the left-controlled National Union of Teachers and the majority of the teachers in the capital, voted to ban police from all schools 'in view of the proven racism of the Metropolitan Police and their inability to deal seriously with racist assaults'.[18]

Understandably the police were anxious to protect themselves against such propaganda, from other members of the race relations network and also from assorted sociologists who appeared ready to assail them whenever opportunity arose. This was not necessarily due to political bias, though sociologists have in modern times tended to be anti-establishment. According to a sharply critical study produced by the Social Affairs Unit,[19] it was more often due to intellectual laziness. For many members of the profession found it easier to accept the stereotype of the police as '"the prejudiced tools of capitalism and racism" (the last two words being practically interchangeable)'. The author, David Waddington, pointed to the large amount of shoddy work, untruths and even refusal to look at the evidence by many of his fellow sociologists who studied crime and police behaviour.

On the whole the police have always accepted that misrepresentation and implacable enmity from political and intellectual radicals are an occupational hazard. Against that they have had better pay and conditions since the arrival in power of Mrs Thatcher. But they have been ill-prepared for the systematic anti-police propaganda which has for some years now not merely been purveyed but *financed* by left-wing local authorities whose sympathies are often openly with those who break rather than with those who enforce the law.

Baroness Cox, who has done valuable work exposing the deliberate left-wing bias introduced into the state schooling sector has become increasingly incensed at the way teenagers in inner-city schools are being urged to resent the police. An example of the sort of subversive literature she had in mind was a glossy cartoon book issued by the Institute of Race Relations on 'How Racism Came to Britain'. Written for youngsters of ten and upwards, 'it is crammed with pictures of Britain as a crude colonial power exclusively concerned with greed and profits. It asserts that British opposition was really motivated not by Christian principles – so much for Wilberforce – but by richer pickings elsewhere.'

More central to our purpose here was a video produced by the GLC and, of course, financed by the ratepayer, called 'Policing London' in which the Communist *Morning Star* figures prominently. 'Grossly one-sided, it shows the police as idle, insensitive, blatantly racist, callously indifferent to attacks on women and behaving improperly on a picket-line [thus appealing to] a ragbag of causes.'[20] There were photographs of police manhandling a little boy. A picture of two policemen arresting a young man covered with blood was headed 'A Search for Excitement'. There was no attempt to show that the police had taken criticism of themselves seriously and that the Metropolitan Police Commissioner had recently issued a 'Guidance for Professional Behaviour'.

The video and the cartoon book were linked. Tony Bunyan was then Acting Head of the GLC's police committee support unit and also a leading figure in the Race Relations Institute, where he was a member of the general council and served on the editorial committee of its journal *Race and Class*. The Institute of Race

Relations, founded in 1952, had originally been an academic body in good standing, set up to monitor race relations and with such respected bodies as the Ford Foundation providing funds. In 1973, however, the politically impartial and academic constitution was overturned by the staff, the council dismissed and the Institute turned into a Marxist pressure group. It was then that Ambalvaner Sivanandan from Sri Lanka became its Director. He had a leading role in the publication of the pamphlet which gives such a grotesquely distorted picture of the British among whom he made his home. The change in the character of the institute alarmed the sponsors and the money dried up until Ken Livingstone's GLC rescued it with hundreds of thousands of pounds of ratepayers' cash. This enabled it to obtain comfortable offices in London's Leeke Street from which to carry on its apparent mission of making race relations worse.[21]

The subsequent dissolution of the GLC did not, unhappily, end the anti-police campaign waged at local government level. The Inner London boroughs of Lambeth, Haringey, Islington, etc. continued where the GLC left off. Thus Lambeth borough council was reported in January 1987 to be telling its staff not on any account to allow council property to be used for surveillance operations by the police, or to divulge information to them from council files.[22] Another example of council refusal to co-operate with the police was so extreme as to merit the description 'sabotage'. This was a poster campaign undertaken in May 1987 by another police monitoring group in the London borough of Lewisham – Lewisham Action on Policing. The aim of the group, which by then had been in existence for three years, was to discourage blacks from joining the police. One of its brightly-coloured posters depicted a black policeman shooting a black woman while a white officer looked on smugly. It was headlined, 'The state wants black recruits to carry out police murders. Don't join the police.' The leaflet continued, 'We all know why the authorities want black people in uniform. They think that they can hide their racism behind a few black faces.' This group was receiving an annual grant of £64,000 from Lewisham borough council. Although the council disassociated itself from this poster, Chris Boothman, the chairman of Action on Policing's management committee, said he did not regret it. Senior worker Amajit Singh, whom the *Sunday Times* photographed proudly displaying the poster, was reported as saying, 'The police are considered the enemy by many blacks and I consider them the enemy. Blacks should not be tempted to join the police.'[23]

Among other anti-police monitoring groups in London was Greenwich Action Committee Against Racial Attacks (GACARA). This too was funded by the rates through an £80,000 grant from Greenwich council, which was Labour-controlled.

Ideas have consequences. Sow among the younger generation of blacks the belief that the police are racist, and it is just a matter of time before not only the police themselves but the whole system of law and order which protects both black and white comes under threat.

On Sunday 8 September 1985 it was carnival time in the racially mixed Handsworth district of Birmingham and the festivities were launched by no other than the city's Chief Constable. Yet many of those who were happily dancing to steel bands that evening were, twenty-four hours later, dancing round the flames of a neighbourhood on fire. The whole thing began with a trivial incident when a Rastafarian motorist was challenged by a policeman over his vehicle's out-of-date licence. When eventually the policeman attempted to arrest the driver over a hundred black youths appeared and he and colleagues who had subsequently joined him came under attack. This was the start of a full-scale riot in the course of which the police suffered heavy casualties, dozens of buildings were looted and destroyed, £5 million of damage was done and two Asian shopkeepers who kept the local sub-post office died.[24]

A report on the disturbances for the local council by the former MP Julius Silverman concluded that unemployment, deprivation and race discrimination were the causes of the riot.[25] Another report for the West Midlands county council was chaired by Herman Ouseley, assistant chief executive of Lambeth borough council. It also blamed deprivation. In addition it spoke of the 'day-to-day' oppression of the blacks and a bitter history of conflict between the local community and the police.[26] The local Labour MPs like Jeff Rooker had no more time for this nonsense than the Home Secretary, Douglas Hurd, who roundly condemned the riot as the work of 'criminal elements'. The police/community relations in this area had until then been quite good, which was one reason why the police were taken by surprise. The people who did regard the police as the enemy were local drug-dealers. They had begun with marketing cannabis but had moved over to selling heroin and cocaine in the street on a colossal scale and were frightened of the police cracking down. The riot was their response to police interference with their lucrative trade.[27] Needless to say the huge damage caused by the riot meant that the deprivation and unemployment from which the community suffered became palpably worse.

On 5 October 1985, during a raid on her home in Tottenham, Mrs Cynthia Jarrett, a respected figure in the local black community, was knocked over by a police officer and died of a heart attack despite efforts by the police to revive her. As a result the police were expecting trouble from resentful blacks from the enormous local housing estate, Broadwater Farm, but their guess was that it might take the form of a Brixton-style riot in the nearby shopping centre of Wood Green. Instead the police themselves were attacked on the Broadwater Estate. Attacks on police vehicles sent to pen the youths inside the estate soon turned into a full-scale clash of arms in which the police were at first heavily outnumbered and assailed by showers of missiles and petrol bombs. These were in such plentiful supply that many must have been prepared in advance. The situation was made worse by ambushes made easy by numerous overhead pathways on the estate. The police sustained heavy casualties and, in the worst incident of all, Police Constable Blakelock was hacked to death. According to one witness, the crowd surrounded him like vultures pecking at something on the ground. When his body was eventually recovered it bore forty stabs or cuts, and one six-inch gash in his cheek fractured and splintered the lower jaw.

The Metropolitan Police Commissioner later admitted that many technical mistakes had been committed in dealing with the riots. For instance the officers there were not trained to use plastic bullets. Yet the main fault was not technical but in the approach. The Broadwater Farm had become a textbook example of community policing and top priority had been given to forging links between people and police. But in practice, it had become a case of doing deals with bully boys and hardened criminals like Winston Silcotts, the man who played the leading role in the murder of PC Blakelock, for which he was tried and sent to gaol. As a result of this appeasement approach, according to a survey by three criminologists, half the women and one in seven of the men on the estate were frightened to go out after dark. In her scathing report written after the riot, Sergeant Gillian Meynell, who was in charge of the home-beat team, said she was ordered to brief her officers at the time of the Broadwater Farm festival in August 1985 to do nothing about the drugs they saw in order not to antagonize the black youths.[28] She also claimed that a week before the riot petrol bombs were being made and young blacks were having throwing practice. Despite police denials the estate had become, for a good deal of the time, a no-go area.

These two riots were moments of truth. Thereafter, the softly-softly policy made fashionable by the Scarman Report began to give ground to the traditional view: the enforcement of law and order must always come first.

7

Inner City Innocence

A fish is said to rot first in the head but a city's decay starts at the heart. The declining inner city is a widespread feature of our time, experience of which for the ethnic minorities has been uniquely direct.

Of course, Britain's city centres have been on the wane for decades, ever since the railway and motor car made it easy for the upper and middle classes to move out of town to the country or to semi-rural suburbia and commute. The substantial houses in which they had formerly lived either became offices, mute and lifeless after working hours, or, after being divided up, apartments, rented to the teeming poor. Often, though, the rents which could be charged were too low to finance proper maintenance and the buildings gradually deteriorated into slums. War and bombing in many cases added devastation to decay, though control of rents at uneconomic levels wrought still greater havoc by ensuring that proper maintenance was counted out. Yet, as long as there was full employment, into the city centres the job-seekers continued to pour. At first came people from the countryside and the villages round about, then from further afield came the immigrants, the last legacies of empire, seeking work, security, and the better life which their British passports virtually guaranteed until the seventies, when the oil embargo precipitated the end of the long post-war world boom and the dole queues grew and grew.

Meanwhile the relentless competitive onslaught of the energetic peoples of the Pacific basin was already wiping out much of the traditional manufacturing in our old industrial towns. So factories, functionless and forlorn, and a new legion of ethnic unemployed added to the decay of urban dwellings to create the economic decline which lies at the heart of the inner-city problem today.

Economic decadence was all-pervasive: as the springs of prosperity dried up, so the quality of the public services went down. The best teachers, doctors, dentists, not to mention social workers, firemen and policemen preferred to work in leafy Surrey among the well-to-do rather than in Inner London's crumbling Hackney among the poor. No wonder then that the centres of many of Britain's great cities became wastelands of crime, depravity, misery and hopelessness, and that, in this wretched scenario, the ethnic minorities, lacking the knowledge and familiarity with the English language which would enable them to adapt, fared, or appeared to fare, worst of all. Indeed the contention of their spokesmen is that the ethnic minorities in the inner cities are 'a permanently trapped population of poor persons'.

Most of those who regularly ventilate their views on television, in the press or from the pulpit, see this inner-city ruin in the same terms as the Commission of Race Equality, that is as the inevitable consequence of a capitalist economy. On the basis of such a diagnosis it was perhaps inevitable that the prescription would be costly state action. Public money was to be used to create jobs, replace slum tenements and sink schools and to pay the salaries of experts on urban social problems. Among the latter would be numerous race relations supervisors to ensure through positive action that the treatment of the ethnics was fair.

Here I shall take issue with this diagnosis and prescription, first by questioning the evidence behind the claim that the ethnics constitute a deprived underclass among the other inner-city dwellers. I shall then challenge the above commonly held analysis of the causes of the inner cities' woes. I shall try to show that the policy proposals based upon it will not alleviate the condition of the inhabitants. Rather, by putting them into a state of increased dependency, encouraging the universal excuse that their troubles are all due to racism and by destroying the family unit which is the anchor of self-reliance, it will make the ethnics' last position worse than their first. As an alternative approach I shall elaborate the idea that the inner city's present afflictions are mainly due to an excess of municipal socialism, planning and controls, which is aggravated by the dependency culture fostered by the welfare state. The solution must therefore be sought through their reduction. The inner cities' most urgent need is not more state intervention but less.

Let's begin however by looking at one of the most exhaustive statements of the orthodox view I reject. It is the Report of the Archbishop of Canterbury's Commission on Urban Priority Areas, called 'Faith in the City', which was published in 1985.[1] Its importance is not due to the quality of its thinking, which is not high, but to its being so typical of the average educated person's view: it is a mirror of current shibboleths.

Considering its provenance it is perhaps not surprising that the report is an indictment of capitalist society and an attack on government economic policy for 'widening the gap between rich and poor'. It complains of the growing number of inner-city folk 'excluded by poverty or powerlessness from sharing in the common life of the nation' ('powerlessness' here seems to mean exactly the same as 'poverty'); elsewhere it remarks that they 'are forced to live on the margins of poverty or below the threshold of an acceptable standard of living'.

The Tory MPs like Peter Bruinvels and John Carlisle who criticized the document at the time were widely accused of overreacting when they called it 'Marxist'.[2] Yet it is riddled with economism – the distinctively Marxist idea that economic conditions are crucial and determine all else in society: culture, religion, personal relationships and politics. In this particular case it takes the form, slightly naïve from a Marxist point of view, of making an individual's 'power' a simple question of his or her share of the Gross Domestic Product. It goes on to talk of the 'wider question' concerning 'the structure of our society', and asserts darkly that, 'The exclusion of the poor is pervasive and not accidental. It is organized by powerful institutions which represent the rest of us.' This bears a strong family resemblance to the anti-racism lobby's 'institutionalized racism' and it performs the same function of seeking to impose on society a collective sense of guilt. For, though the report goes on to call for a pledge to a deeper commitment, this is less a demand made upon the individual personally to undertake to help the inner-city poor – that would be an appeal with genuine moral content – but to support the political aim of creating 'a society in which benefits and burdens are shared in a more equitable way'. Shorn of the verbiage this is just another plea for the redistribution of income through higher taxation. In some eyes the Church of England's stance was out-and-out hypocrisy. Conservative MP Terry Dicks said, 'I am amazed that the Archbishop should make these comments bearing in mind that he heads an organization, the Church Commissioners, which is one of the worst landlords London has ever seen.'[3]

Fifteen out of the twenty-three proposals call for increased government expenditure. They urge more spending on the Rate Support Grant, the urban programme, voluntary bodies, small firms, job creation, relaxed eligibility rules for claimants, an expanded Community Programme, Supplementary Benefit, Child Benefit, higher earnings disregards, a bigger public housing programme, assistance for the homeless, the handicapped, law centres and community work.[4] Their other principal suggestions are that mortgage tax relief should be abandoned in order to create more money for redistribution and that more police activity in the inner city would be 'counter-productive'.

Thus the Church of England researchers, like many members of the race relations industry,[5] are keen to promote the belief that ethnic minorities are the worst casualties of the inner city. Yet, though in some respects many of them are indeed worse off than the members of the host community, as Geoffrey Parkins puts it in his section of the pamphlet 'Reversing Racism', 'The majority of Britain's ethnic minorities are employed, well-housed, educated and moving up the social ladder.'[6]

As regards employment Parkins cites evidence that the proportion of economically active blacks is slightly higher than that of whites, and that the majority are satisfied with their jobs. Of the Asians the ratio in unskilled jobs is not much different from that of whites. Since Parkins wrote, the unemployment position seems to have worsened: in spring 1985 it was 10 per cent for whites, 21 per cent among West Indians, 17 per cent among Indians and 31 per cent among Pakistanis and Bangladeshis. This however is partly because the ethnic groups have a low age profile and are afflicted disproportionately by heavy unemployment among the younger age groups. In other words they are particularly vulnerable to high minimum wage levels which put the young and inexperienced at a disadvantage by pricing them out of jobs. The geographical concentration of ethnic minorities in the inner-city areas and their occupational concentration in manufacturing which has been shedding labour in recent years are other contributory factors. On the positive side, however, grasp of the English language among ethnics should improve and this should help their employment prospects. Again, a larger percentage of the minority groups have higher qualifications than whites (18.3 against 13.4 per cent) and this too holds hope for the future. Finally, the share of the Asian population which is self-employed is much higher than for whites or blacks and it is especially in this self-employed, small business sector that new jobs are being created.[7]

As for wages, Parkins showed that in both semi-skilled and unskilled work, minority groups earned more than whites, while incomes for minority women were higher at all levels.

In housing, contrary to received sociological wisdom, ethnics have done quite well. In 1971, 76 per cent of Asians, and 50 per cent of West Indians owned their own homes, compared with 50 per cent of the white population. The Commission for Racial Equality, noting the growth in owner-occupation among the Asians, commented sourly that it meant that Asians were being forced in many cases to buy older terrace houses because of low incomes, exclusion from council and private rented property and the need to service large loans at high rates of interest. This was bound, it added, to result in 'an inability to instal basic amenities' which proved that the Asian community had a 'severe housing need'. All that it in fact proved was that the Commission for Racial Equality is capable of finding a problem in every solution. For, as a 1977 survey showed, 82 per cent of Asian and West Indian households were satisfied and 45 per cent very satisfied with their homes. Many of them bought their houses through hard work, often at considerable sacrifice of other amenities of life and often by crowding in tenants to find income enough to pay off the mortgage. Yet they are now quite rightly reaping the reward which, since the recent explosive rise in house prices, has become very considerable.

Further research by sociologist J.G. Davies and his students in 1984 showed that the CRE's surmise was groundless. Interviewing fifty-four Asian households in Newcastle, Davies found a 'lack of a desire for council housing, an absence of any compulsion to use bank loans, an absence of structural racialism and discrimination, whether by local authority or private provider; and, overwhelmingly . . . [a] resolute refusal of the Asian population to take on the role of a downtrodden sub-proletariat, forced into the grotty end of a dual housing market.' Davies concludes that the notion of Asian households being the passive victims of systematic racial discrimination, as many of his fellow sociologists assert, is nonsense.[8]

One uncomfortable fact for those who attribute all differences in group achievement to racial discrimination is the much better academic performance of Asians than West Indians. The view taken by some psychologists, that blacks are less intelligent, as their consistently low average scores in IQ tests are held to prove, is unconvincing, because a significant number of blacks do much better than whites. Moreover the fact that black children in America who are adopted by white parents raise their IQ by about fifteen points suggests that much of the poor performance of blacks in IQ tests is not hereditary but cultural and therefore capable of being improved through changes in the social and indeed political environment. American blacks have been scoring more in IQ tests since the triumph of the civil rights campaign led by Martin Luther King, though it is intriguing that the descendants of those negroes who were 'free persons of colour' before the American civil war still have higher IQs than the rest.

An ingenious theory put forward by Professor Alan Little (Lewisham Professor of Social Administration, University of London) in a broadcast talk republished in *Five Views of Multi-Racial Britain* by the CRE in 1978, is that the superior educational attainment of Asians stems from their having a strong culture of which they are proud, while the West Indians are part of the dominant culture which is rejecting them. The latter, he claims, have nothing to fall back on psychologically, and this undermines their intellectual development. Yet the superiority of the Asian culture in adapting to British society may consist of no more than what we might literally call their urbanity, that is their familiarity with town life. The poor educational performance of many of the American blacks in North American cities is due to their having come recently from rural communities in the Deep South; it may take them a couple of generations to adapt. In any case, since the West Indians belong to the dominant British culture their best hope of succeeding in life is to embrace that culture.

Whether or not under the influence of Professor Little's theory, in 1979 the then Secretary of State for Education, Mrs Shirley Williams, set up an enquiry into the very poor educational achievement of West Indian children. A survey of school-leavers by her ministry showed indeed that Asian and white pupils did between twice and six times as well as West Indian pupils at O-level and six times better at A-level. Mr Anthony Rampton, who was in the chair, was anxious to submit a unanimously approved report and went out of his way to avoid any explanation which could be regarded as 'racist'. Thus his multi-racial committee found in an interim report published in June 1981 that the causes of West Indian under-achievement were mainly racism, negative teacher attitudes and an inappropriate curriculum. This explanation was patently absurd, for it failed to account for the fact that the Asians, who suffered just as much from racial discrimination, not only performed better than the West Indians but in many respects better than the whites. It turned out that the committee had suppressed intriguing evidence that nearly twice as many West Indian mothers went out to work as Asian mothers and that the incidence of single-parent families among West Indians was thirteen times higher.[9]

Rampton was subsequently dismissed, and Lord Swann, former chairman of the BBC, drafted in instead but he fared no better. A £78,000 research programme into black family structures which the committee tried to establish through the Inner London Education Authority ran into opposition from minority pressure groups and had to be abandoned. The provenance of Lord Swann's fellow committee members did not augur well for the final report: they included Mr Peter Newsam, who left it to take up his appointment as chairman of the Commission for Racial Equality, and Mrs Ann Dummet, author of *A Portrait of English Racism* and later director of the Runnymede Trust. Mrs Dummet resigned because she disagreed with the way Lord Swann had redrafted the chapter on under-achievement. Even so the final document was no advance on its interim predecessor except in length. It stretched to 1,000 pages, and cost £700,000. Once more ignoring the fact that Asians were as subject to racial discrimination as the West Indians it attributed the poor educational performance of the latter to racism both in the schools and in society at large. It then made seventy-three recommendations for curing the malady which it had incorrectly diagnosed. These included the abolition of Christian morning prayers in school because they are meaningless to Muslims and Hindus and a proposal that every school, even those in all-white areas, should be required to provide courses in Punjabi, Gujerati and Creole.[10] These absurd proposals are mentioned only to demonstrate the cast of mind of such 'experts' on race questions. The Swann Report was a dismal failure which botched the answer to the question it was posed. For it is quite clear from the success of the Asians in British schools that, as a factor in educational under-achievement, racism is not significant.

Nobody disputes that many members of the ethnic minorities labour under grievous disadvantages. Though they are far from being modern versions of the downtrodden and exploited Helots in Sparta, many of them, especially those who live in the inner cities, are, compared with the rest of the community, considerably worse off. But to attribute this to white racism is to ignore the several other and more important factors at work.

Prominent among these is municipal socialism. Its malign influence goes far to explain the fact already referred to that areas like Brixton and Toxteth, which are said to exhibit the inner city's afflictions in the most extreme form, and which have certainly seen the worst rioting in recent times, have received most government aid – far beyond anything allocated to the Continent's major industrial towns. The explanation of this paradox is that the way the aid has been used has made it less an answer to the problems than a part of it. For most of the money went into comprehensive redevelopment. Old city centres, many of them proud legacies of their Victorian heyday, together with convenient and economic terraced housing, were demolished to make way for modern civic and shopping centres, usually high-rise offices, commercial buildings and flats. As the *Economist* put it, with particular reference to London: 'These redevelopments have had a devastating impact on the sort of employment – workshops, servicing and small manufacturing firms – most receptive to black labour. One estimate suggested over 3,000 jobs may have gone in the clearance schemes in Lambeth alone.'[11]

The grandiose schemes of the planners not only destroy jobs, they remove the people who give leadership to the community. It is the people who have some local standing, those who own their own homes, or run their own small businesses such as shops or pubs or workshops doing repairs, who by being bought out, often

110

by the council using its powers of compulsory purchase, are the first to leave the community. These are the local pillars of society who keep a beady eye on the youth of the district and tick off youngsters or report them to their parents if they misbehave. Once these solid citizens have gone, what is left is a rootless population amid a landscape of derelict property waiting to be knocked down. Very often the council, having run out of money, postpones the development, perhaps for good, and the buildings are vandalized or, if there is a riot, burned to the ground.

Municipal socialism also removes jobs by raising rates and driving out businesses. Professor Patrick Minford of the University of Liverpool recently calculated that if business rates on Merseyside had risen since 1974 by only the same amount as elsewhere, unemployment in this racially mixed area would be three per cent lower. He also claimed that it is mathematically demonstrable that, of the nine regions of England and Wales, those with above average rate increases had higher unemployment as a consequence. A more concrete illustration of the point is the comparison of two London boroughs, Wandsworth and Lambeth, which have much the same population, in each case including a large ethnic element. They are adjacent and similar neighbour-hoods on the south side of the Thames. The difference is that Wandsworth has had a Conservative administration since 1978 which has kept the rates down, while Lambeth has been ruled in the same period by extravagant members of the hard left who have recklessly hoisted them up: Wandsworth's rates have risen by three-fifths, Lambeth's have increased more than threefold. Lambeth's unemployment has throughout been higher than Wandsworth's, but the telling evidence is that the margin has steadily widened. Thus, while Lambeth had 40 per cent more unemployed than Wandsworth in 1979, by the beginning of 1987 the gap had grown to 60 per cent.[12]

Socialist councils have in the past been especially keen on high-rise blocks of flats, although, as the American writer Jane Jacobs pointed out a quarter of a century ago with regard to similar huge developments in the USA, they undermine the feeling of community. This is because the segregation of all land uses into large units leads to all the amenities – grounds, parks, schools, shopping precincts, industrial estates and cultural com-plexes – being excessively big. As a result few destinations are

111

within walking distance, people go everywhere by car and get little chance to make acquaintances, let alone friends. Jane Jacobs believed that this lack of human scale, combined with the high-rise style of architecture which gave little chance for people to keep an eye open for strangers, created a feeling of insecurity which had a devastating effect, especially on children. A decade later this idea was taken further by Oscar Newman in his famous book *Defensible Space*. He showed that many high-rise designs which won architectural awards had a great deal of anonymous public space in corridors, walkways and numerous entrances. By providing easy escape routes for evildoers, these fostered crime. Because nobody owned them, public hallways, passageways and lifts positively invited the graffiti artist to do his worst. Mothers ten floors up not only could not watch out for crooks or muggers; they could not watch out for their children playing outside as they would if they had a garden in a normal house. Young children whose flat was high up often did not get home to urinate in time and did so in the lifts which then began to stink. These ideas have been investigated in detail by research into literally thousands of apartment blocks by Alice Coleman and her team from the Land Use Research Unit of King's College, London. By her criteria it is clear that blocks like Tottenham's Broadwater Farm Estate were almost doomed from the start to become centres of crime, vandalism and riot.

The truly awful character of many of these estates was brought home to the British public in 1968. After a gas explosion at Ronan Point, a twenty-one-storey tower block in East London, there followed what was aptly described at the time as 'progressive collapse'. The combination of poor buildings and the damage wreaked by their inhabitants meant that in many cases there was no alternative to demolition. One such tower block in Hackney in East London has ended its life in a series of controlled explosions. At least 10,000 dwellings built since 1970 have been torn down. Here is another example of where we might have learnt from American mistakes instead of repeating them painfully at great cost ourselves.

The most notorious, because the most appalling, of these high-rise disasters was an enormous architectural-prize-winning project called Pruitt-Igoe, built in St Louis, Missouri in 1955. Physically it deteriorated fast and was soon plagued by vandalism, crime and drugs. In 1971 those still left in it were invited to a meeting and for the first time actually asked what they wanted to be done with the estate. They responded with the chant 'Blow it . . . *up*.' They were taken at their word and the block was dynamited the following year.[13]

The relevance of this to the ethnic community in Britain is that these are the sorts of council blocks in which the West Indians in particular tend to get trapped. This at least was the conclusion the Commission for Racial Equality drew from its study of race and council housing in Hackney. Conducted in the late seventies, its researches found that, while the West Indians (the majority group among the ethnics there) were allocated their fair overall share of council accommodation, whites were generally awarded the better houses and maisonettes. The West Indians were for the most part consigned to dilapidated pre-war flats and even more dilapidated post-war tower blocks (like the one that was later demolished). Predictably this was taken to be a plain case of 'institutionalized racism', but the evidence can be plausibly read in quite a different way.

An alternative explanation starts from the assumption, well grounded in experience, that the people who get the best flats (indeed the best anything else which is obtained from the authorities and involves successfully negotiating with bureaucrats) are those who are most articulate, that is, generally speaking, the better-educated. These are usually members of the middle or better-off working classes. Intriguingly, according to the CRE's own report, only 12 per cent of whites in Hackney were owner-occupiers while for the West Indians the figure was 26 per cent. For other ethnics the percentage was higher still – Africans 35 per cent and Asians 48 per cent. It is thus likely that the better-educated, better-off whites devoted themselves to acquiring the pick of the council's houses or maisonettes or ground-floor flats. The better-educated, more prosperous West Indians, Asians and Africans, on the other hand, didn't bother with renting from the council but bought houses or flats on mortgages. If this is indeed what happened, considering how property prices have rocketed, the ethnic owner-occupiers have come off best. Moreover, it is possible that the West Indian council tenants have fared no worse than the whites of similar education and income in the quality of dwelling they have obtained. If the CRE is right in saying that Hackney, in its policy until recently of discrimination against non-whites, was typical of the country as a whole, the paradoxical conclusion may be that such 'institutionalized racism' actually works to the detriment of whites.

Yet, supposing that ethnics do suffer from discrimination practised by local authorities, that does not necessarily prove the need for a campaign against racism in town halls. An alternative inference might be that, if racism is widespread in borough housing departments, local councils should not be entrusted with the landlord's role. Why don't the CRE, the Runnymede Trust and the Institute of Race Relations campaign for council house sales? For when it comes to buying as opposed to renting from the council, no distinction is made between ethnic money and white. Of course, even to ask such a question is to invite a ribald response. For the race relations professionals have no interest in dissolving racial problems by axeing any branch of officialdom. They have every interest, though, in highlighting its misbehaviour and calling for the creation or extension of a countervailing bureaucracy whose growth will ensure that their own services are in ever greater demand. That is why the race relations quango-crats, ready as they are to criticize racist conduct in local government, will always be the last to urge that its role be reduced.

Welfarism, because of its destructive effect on the family, is also ultimately harmful to the ethnic minorities' prospects. As in America, it does most damage to minorities where the family bond is already weak. Take the problem of single-parent families, which, as Lord Scarman mentioned in his report, was a back-ground factor in the situation at Brixton, though one of which he did not make a great deal. For to do so might divert attention from his argument's general thrust that it was on society in general rather than on blacks in particular that the real blame for the disturbances lay. Indeed, it was not the West Indian matriarchal extended family which he saw as a source of social fragility and potential unrest but the impact of English social conditions upon it. The facts in any case were intriguing. As he noted,

> The percentage of children in care and of single-parent families in the black community is noticeably higher than one would expect in relation to the proportion of black people in the community as a whole. Fifty per cent of single-parent families in

the borough of Lambeth in 1978 were non-white. The two wards where the April disorders were centred – Tulse Hill and Herne Hill – contain some 22 per cent of all the single-parent families in Lambeth and 2.1 per cent of the 0–18 age group in those wards are in care. Of the 185 children in care in those two wards on 10 September 1980, 112 (61 per cent) were black.[14]

These facts are probably of crucial importance in explaining the social breakdown which a riot represents. There is ample research evidence which shows that the absence of a father is extremely harmful to a child's moral and mental growth. Sociologist Patricia Morgan, in a *Daily Telegraph* feature article,[15] refers to a study of West Indian, Indian and white children which showed that, while Indians were more likely than whites to enter the professions, few West Indians even got a GCE O-level and that their IQs declined during their time at school. The reason for this, she inferred, was that West Indian children were far more likely to come from fatherless homes. Lack of a father appears to be a significant contributary factor to intellectual backwardness and criminality in all parts of the population. The corollary is that fathers who involve themselves with their children stimulate educational achievement and respect for the law.

Why do West Indians have so many fatherless families? it is often alleged to have something to with the legacy of slavery, which, especially in the West Indies (as opposed to the southern states of America, where slave families were the norm) was inimical to family life. While the loose family arrangement may have been workable in the West Indies, where there was an extended network of kinship, according to research by Juliet Cheetham,[16] in Lambeth such a network did not exist. In any event the West Indian family in Britain is not as strong an institution as it is among whites and certainly weaker than it is among Asians. And, *pace* Lord Scarman, it has not been 'the impact of British social conditions' but exposure to the British welfare state which has wreaked havoc upon it.

Our system of welfare payments has long targeted one-parent families because poverty is chronically concentrated in them. The same problem has arisen as in America: humane and well-meaning attempts to aid the able-bodied poor have had very perverse results. In this case an incentive has been created for young girls to have babies out of wedlock. The girl who wants to leave home but has no wish to work can qualify for a council flat and enough benefits to get by if she becomes pregnant. That is why, in the population as a whole, the number of unmarried mothers has doubled in the last thirty years. It is not surprising that, if these are the effects of our welfare system on the population in general, the impact on the West Indians with their feebler family structure has been more demoralizing still.

Lord Scarman referred to the large number of black children in care, a continuing problem which is aggravated by the misguided campaign against the adoption of black children by white foster-parents which 'anti-racists' now conduct. One of the grounds for their opposition is that whites cannot furnish the black child with the 'coping-mechanisms' which they claim blacks have to learn in order to survive in our allegedly 'racist' society. The other main argument is that adoption by whites will make the child lose its black identity, and that this amounts to cultural genocide.

Yet an authoritative study of mixed-race adoption in America by Joyce Lardner, a black sociologist from the Deep South, concluded that 'there are many whites who are capable of rearing emotionally healthy black children',[17] and there is plenty of other evidence that black children adjust well in white homes. There is also the curious discovery in tests carried out at the University of Minnesota that black children adopted by whites have IQs fifteen points above the average achieved by other black children in the same area.[18]

Yet, despite these obvious advantages and the arguments of common humanity and commonsense, white adoption of black children is being stopped by politically motivated people, either ruling or administering, in local authorities up and down the land. This policy, which robs numerous black children in care of a decent start in life, disturbs the conscience of many social workers, but for fear of being called 'racist' they are unwilling to protest.

To sum up, the condition of the run-down inner cities and the plight of the ethnic minorities in them are two of the most pressing problems in Britain today. Yet there is no question of there being an ethnic underclass. The real picture is a mixed one. The Asians, for instance (who represent about half the total number hailing from the countries of the New Commonwealth), though some groups of them suffer severe unemployment, are markedly

116

successful in buying their own houses, in setting up their own businesses and in the educational attainment of their youth. These developments obviously hold promise for the future. The problem of ethnic poverty in the inner cities is primarily a problem of the quarter of the total who are of West Indian origin, and especially a problem of West Indian youth. Yet there are hopeful signs. According to the Eggleston Report on the educational and vocational experiences of young black people, summarized in a research report published by the Runnymede Trust (1987), Afro-Caribbean pupils are more likely to believe that it is important to do well in school than white pupils and also have higher aspirations. Again, Afro-Caribbean mothers are, it seems, 'considerably more likely than any other group of parents to go to schools to discuss their children's future job or career. Indeed, given their probable greater likelihood of working full-time and perhaps working shiftwork, their diligence when compared with other parents is particularly noteworthy.'

The fact that the Asians are higher achievers in almost all respects and in education especially outdo the whites shows that these troubles cannot mainly be due to racial discrimination. It may be more to the point to estimate how much racial discrimination in jobs is ironically the result of the activities of the CRE and associated bodies. For there is no question that they often frighten off potential employers who feel that, if they take on an ethnic worker, to dismiss him even for the best of reasons is to risk being accused of racial discrimination and landing up with all the bother and expense of an appearance in court. Moreover, much of what passes for racial discrimination is better described as lack of acculturation; that is, ethnics have not yet sufficiently adapted to British ways. In the ordinary course of events that should change for the better. But things will not get better if the ethnics go down the blind alleys of aggressive cultural chauvinism and chronic welfare dependency mapped out by the race relations lobby and the Labour left. It is not heartless but practical to advise black youth in particular not to start out in life by looking to authority for help. The *Economist* recently offered all young Americans who want to avoid poverty some advice which makes universal sense. It was (a) Complete high school (b) Get and stay married and (c) Get a job even at a very low wage and stay in it.[19]

Of course it is hard to follow the last crucial bit of advice if you live in a run-down inner-city area where jobs are very scarce. What is needed to make the formula work is the restoration of private enterprise; up till now municipal socialism has stood in the way. It is also necessary, if blacks are to find it easier to get jobs, for them to acquire marketable skills. Here the obstacles have been stick-in-the-mud teachers' unions and left-wing local authorities who are trying to push politics into the classroom at the expense of learning.

If present Conservative plans go forward these barriers to the progress of blacks should be removed. Urban development corporations, on the pattern of the one that has already worked so well in London's docklands, should provide the right framework in which the government's various other schemes for fostering enterprises large and small and for extending youth training in tandem, will prosper. Similarly, in education, the tightening up of standards and the option offered to parents and school governors to take their schools out of local authority control should at last break the stranglehold of those councils who have held back educational advance for so long. All this depends on political reform, to the racial aspects of which we now turn.

8

The False Promise of Politics

To the race relations lobby (and indeed to many others who have not had the time or opportunity to study the matter) the importance of political activity in exorcizing the problems of race seems self-evident. For instance, in his book *Race and Politics*, Muhammad Anwar, the Research Director of the Commission for Racial Equality, took as his theme the proposition, 'Participation in the political process by the ethnic minorities is essential in achieving equality of opportunity.'[1] Yet, obvious to the point of triteness as this may seem, it is nevertheless not true.

Participation by ethnic minorities in this country's politics is indeed desirable, but not because it will necessarily further their prosperity (though that could be the indirect result). Rather it is desirable because each individual member of those minorities is entitled to become an elector and joining in political activity is a corollary. It is what everyone owes to this country as his or her due for belonging to it. That we do not all take this obligation for granted is one of the corrupting effects of the welfare state. In post-Beveridge Britain we have tended more and more to think of membership of our democracy as a ticket, entitling the holder to join in a squalid scramble for benefits, instead of as a privilege, a share in a decent and just, even a great, society, enabling – indeed requiring – its possessor to contribute to the common good. All of us, the ethnic minorities included, need to give new life to the concept of citizenship frankly put by Pericles in his funeral oration: 'We regard a man who takes no interest in public affairs, not as a harmless but as a useless character; and if few of us are originators, we are all sound judges of a policy.' If that part of the speech is remembered too rarely, another admonition of his we seem to have forgotten altogether: 'To avow poverty is no disgrace; the true disgrace is in doing nothing to avoid it.'[2]

The democratic tradition puts far more stress on what its people can contribute to society than on what society can do for them. This is no doubt because, in the past, people were more conscious of how lucky they were to enjoy freedom, peace and security under the rule of law. These fundamental but nowadays often unappreciated advantages of living in a democracy can themselves be put at risk if its citizens expect to withdraw more from the system while contributing less.

In questioning the efficacy of the political route to ethnic economic improvement let us first refer back to the chapter on lessons from America. There it was pointed out that the racial minorities like the Japanese and the Chinese who, despite the disgraceful and humiliating racial discrimination initially practised against them by the authorities, deliberately kept politics at arms' length, are now at the top of the US incomes league. The North American Indians, on the other hand, who have devoted more of their energies to political campaigning as a means of improving their group material welfare than any other ethnic group, are the poorest of them all. This is not because their political pressure has failed, for by any criterion it has succeeded beyond all expectation. Yet the results have been ruinous beyond belief. For all who seek what they consider their economic deserts through exclusively political channels it is a cautionary tale, the details of which are worth spelling out.

Of the million and a half people who claim Indian origin in the USA about half live on or near one of the 260 reservations. Each reservation is independent, with its own system of law, government and leaders. These Indians have enjoyed special status since 1871 when Congress made them wards of state. Now, under twenty different federal programmes, they receive around $3 billion a year purely for being who they are. This includes free medical, hospital, dental and optical treatment and considerable 'tribal payments'. They are provided with free legal services and free education up to PhD level. Those who live on a reservation pay no state or federal taxes whatsoever on land, or income derived from it, nor licence duty on their car. On the reservation they are allowed to sell, for use elsewhere, fireworks which are illegal outside its boundaries. They are even permitted to fish and hunt without a licence regardless of the seasonal and bag restrictions which apply to all other Americans, and to sell what they kill. Yet according to American sociologist Ted Williams:

> American Indians have the highest infant mortality rate, the shortest life span, the poorest housing, the poorest transportation, the lowest *per capita* income, and the lowest level of education in the nation. In 1985 the Bureau of Indian Affairs reported that the unemployment rate on reservations had reached 49 per cent. Other sources say it is even higher. When last the government checked, approximately 400,000 Indians (that is one fourth of the Indian population, or 40 per cent of those on reservations) lived below the poverty level – more than twice the proportion among the general population. No ethnic group in America has lower average income than the Indians. Suicide and alcoholism are epidemic. The rate of alcohol-related deaths among Indians is 5.6 times that of the general population.[3]

The independence of the tribes is jealously preserved, but this only delivers most of the reservation Indians into the hands of tyrannical and corrupt tribal leaders who terrorize them into submission. So largely as a result of lobbying which took advantage of the American people's sense of guilt, these Indians have been subjected to 'the twin burdens of economic socialism and political despotism' and are the country's most oppressed minority. In 1984 the mainly Indian Presidential Commission on Indian Reservation Economics concluded in its report that 'One of the major obstacles to Indian economic progress is the United States Government.' Its authors spoke with unintended irony. For the US government, by making them totally dependent on federal assistance and taking away every challenge in their lives has created the biggest possible obstacle to the Indians' economic, or for that matter moral, advance. It is a tragic illustration of the perverse effect of governmental benevolence.

Those who find this lesson from across the Atlantic unpalatable may object that the experience of the Red Indians is not a valid guide because it is too far removed from our own. In response let us take an example from nearer home, namely the racial politics of Liverpool, which has been the subject of a lively recent study by the Runnymede Trust.[4]

Liverpool is a city of half a million with, mainly as a legacy from its past as England's greatest Atlantic port, an ethnic population of 40,000, half of them Liverpool-born blacks but also including Asians, Arabs and Chinese. The Runnymede Trust pamphlet claims that these people, whom it characteristically groups under the heading 'blacks' (including Chinese), have long been the object of severe racial discrimination in jobs, wages, council housing, education and harassment by the police. It describes how a campaign was organized, though it is presented as a more or less spontaneous protest from local democratic ethnic minority organizations, to obtain Liverpool city council's official support for the promotion of an equal opportunities policy. This was accepted by the Liberals when they were in power in the early eighties with very little result. The real story begins when the Liberals were succeeded by a Labour administration under the control of the Militant Tendency, the fanatical Trotskyite faction with its own organization, agents and finances (some of them allegedly provided by Libya's Colonel Gaddafi), which has successfully infiltrated many Labour constituencies.

The council's real, though not nominal, leader was the comparatively youthful, dynamic and arrogant Derek Hatton, who ran the city on Tammany Hall lines. His power base was in the unions, who in the Labour party play a big part in nominating candidates for local councils. These unions were in turn manipulated through a number of 'sweetheart' branches directly under the thumb of Militant supporters who delivered the vote when required.

In general 'anti-racism' is a left-wing cause and the Liverpool Militants were quite prepared, like the Liberals before them, to give verbal support to equal opportunities policies, but that was as far as it went. For the Liverpool Militants were on the whole antipathetic to black rights. They also felt themselves threatened by the race relations organizations and with reason: here were rivals for power trying to undermine their system of patronage. It is fairly obvious, even from the Runnymede Trust pamphlet's account, that the attempt to assert black rights in Liverpool was

122

not so much a sudden welling-up of indignation among the oppressed minorities but more of a plot master-minded by the local Community Relations Council and ultimately by the Commission for Racial Equality whose research director, Muhammad Anwar, played a prominent part. In fact it was Muhammad Anwar who appears to have superintended the production and publication of a CRE research report on race and housing in Liverpool in 1984 which showed that 'blacks' were allocated consistently poorer quality council accommodation than the whites.

The CRE-inspired black caucus on the city council's Race Relations Liaison Committee demanded, apparently successfully, the creation of all sorts of race relations posts in Liverpool's town hall. There was to be a Multi-Racial Education Unit with seven new appointments, four more staff for Multi-Racial Further and Higher Education, three ethnic librarians, four ethnic housing liaison officers, a Personnel and Social Services Adviser, a Race Training Officer in the Social Services Department, a central Race and Housing Unit and possibly also a Contract Compliance Unit. On top of that there were demands for the provision of such items as a Muslim Meals on Wheels service, a Chinese Social Work Unit, a Black Social Work Project and a Black Home Help Scheme.

Behind the rhetoric about racial justice the real issue in Liverpool was a struggle for power between the incumbent Militant administration with its tame union support, and the race relations authorities who had mobilized the ethnic groups. It wasn't so much a bid for the control over the relatively few posts listed above as over the thousands of jobs, contracts and huge resources over which the occupants of those posts would eventually exercise control. If all council appointments and handouts were subjected to scrutiny by a race monitoring unit which protested every time blacks appeared to have been discriminated against, the power of the city council's ruling clique to hand out the best council houses, high-salaried appointments, or subsidies to its friends would be seriously constrained. Derek Hatton could see that if nothing was done his empire would collapse. What he did therefore was first to take no action to create any of the race relations posts or programmes which he had approved. Then, finding that this policy of masterly inactivity only stirred the black caucus to increasingly angry protest, he agreed in summer 1984 to establish a Race Relations Unit in the Chief Executive's office, along with a batch of appropriate bureaucratic posts. As the Runnymede pamphlet puts it:

> Little did the caucus realize at the time that the unit was being planned by Labour's Militant leadership not as a mechanism to ensure the implementation of racial equality policies, but as a means for Militant and its allies to assert its total control and power over the black community whose public opposition to aspects of Labour policy and practice was becoming a source of embarrassment and anger to the Labour leadership and an independent political challenge that they had decided to find ways to suppress.[5]

The key appointment was that of Principal Race Relations Adviser. This was duly advertised and, at a meeting chaired by Derek Hatton and with black caucus representatives, a short list of applicants was drawn up. The only hint of the trouble to come was Hatton's insistence on the inclusion of one applicant with virtually no qualifications for the post, a London building contractor by the name of Sampson Bond.

The day for interviews arrived and each candidate was asked a list of questions by Hatton, of which the key question was, 'What are your views on positive discrimination?' To this all but one of the applicants replied that, under existing legislation, positive discrimination is normally unlawful but that there was considerable scope for positive action which they considered essential to any meaningful equal opportunities policy. Sampson Bond, however, said that positive discrimination did not solve problems, was dangerous, led to greater divisions, etc., while on the subject of positive action he said not a word. It was a moment to savour. On the one hand were aspirant race relations experts repeating the official line about positive discrimination being unlawful unless it was called by a different name; on the other was Sampson Bond, gradually revealed as the nominee of the Militant town hall bosses, arguing against discriminatory policies even though the whole basis of the Militants' power in Liverpool was the systematic and corrupt abuse of their authority in order to discriminate in favour of their friends.

Not until the votes were counted did the race relations lobbyists realize that they had been taken for a ride. The five Labour councillors on the committee voted the Militant ticket and chose Sampson Bond. It was a fix, but the race relations people were not going to take it lying down. They picketed, they marched and ultimately they appealed to Labour leader Neil Kinnock. At the time he was worried that the antics of the far left would indentify the Labour party with extremism and lose him the next general election. Of course Militant were too well established at constituency level for him to remove altogether, but the conduct of Liverpool city council provided an opportunity for him publicly to dissociate himself from extremism. He could afford to attack the council because, though it was associated with such militant union causes as the striking miners and the prolonged sit-in by the Cammell Laird workers protesting against redundancies, its policy of nepotism had angered the local government union, NALGO. (The power-base of Hatton and Co rested mainly on other unions, GMBATU and especially the TGWU, which had a policy of devolving power to its branches.) The propaganda which Hatton now unleashed against the race relations organizations in Liverpool could also be represented as 'Militants' war on the black community', and as such elicit widespread support for Kinnock's intervention.

Kinnock's opportunity came when, as part of its solution to the financial crisis its irresponsible policies had brought upon itself, the Liverpool city council attempted to sack the entire council workforce. The Labour leader made a rousing speech at that year's party conference denouncing Liverpool's Militants, which was enthusiastically received by the media. He then set in motion the cumbrous machinery through which Hatton and a few of his Militant supporters were to be expelled. It was arguably pure tokenism: the national organization of the Militant Tendency was as powerful as ever – big enough to hold its conference in the Albert Hall. Moreover, some observers felt that the Labour leader was being inconsistent to the point of hypocrisy. For the Liverpool Militants' contention that black sections were divisive was precisely the one which he himself had endorsed nationally in refusing a separate black organization within the Labour fold.

What this story illustrates is how unreliable politics can be as a means of improving the condition of ethnic minorities. Even the far left, who are supposed to be the most sympathetic section of what is allegedly the least racially prejudiced of Britain's main parties, are capable of thoroughly racist behaviour, in the real not merely the pejorative sense. Meanwhile the moderates, for the moment at least more dominant in the Labour leadership, have been ready to climb on the anti-racist bandwagon only when it suits their wider aims. The Good Book's advice 'Put not your trust in princes' might almost have been formulated with our ethnic minorities in mind.

So, briefly to recapitulate, though this might at first sound surprising, Britain's racial minorities would be ill-advised to look to political action for an improvement in their condition. That is not to suggest that they should not involve themselves in British politics but that they should do so as a duty laid on them as citizens of a democracy, not as a means of lobbying for privileges. For even if they obtained all the protections, reverse discriminations and government subsidies that some of their spokesmen have demanded, the result, as the Red Indian example shows, could well be the exact opposite of what they hope for. Government handouts tend to demoralize the recipients. They create a dependent mentality and smother those urges to achieve which have enabled disadvantaged minorities the world over to leave poverty behind.

What influence can the ethnic groups nowadays exert on the policies of parties and governments? Their leverage, given that the ethnic minorities constitute 2.6 million out of a total population of fifty-six million or nearly 5 per cent of the people of Britain, is certainly not to be despised. It is also the more effective for being concentrated in the inner cities and industrial areas and therefore in a limited number of parliamentary seats. It is estimated that in 1985 there were a hundred constituencies where the ethnic minorities (measured by the number of heads of families who come from the New Commonwealth and Pakistan) were 10 per cent of the population. According to the 1981 census there are fifty-eight constituencies where they are 15 per cent, nineteen where they are 25 per cent and seven where they are over 33 per cent. The ethnic vote is most concentrated in London and the West Midlands, the most striking examples (updated to 1986) being London's Brent South (55.6 per cent) and, in the West Midlands, Birmingham's Ladywood (52 per cent). In such constituencies, of course, there are scores of individual wards, the territorial units for which local councillors are elected, where the ethnic minorities are more concentrated still, the most prominent in this case being the Northcote Ward in the London borough of Ealing, where it is 85.4 per cent.

Population is not the same thing as voting strength, however, and there are various factors which make the ethnic vote less formidable than these figures suggest. For one thing the ethnic groups are younger than the average of the population as a whole and therefore tend to have more of their number below voting age. For another they do not register as assiduously as the rest. When they do register the turnout varies, good in the case of the Asians, poor in that of the West Indians. These factors will change with time, but that cannot be said of the principal restraint upon their power, which is the lack of a 'black' political agenda. That is to say there is no issue of such overwhelming and exclusive importance to the ethnic community as a whole that it takes precedence over all others and sets the community apart from the rest of the electorate.

Opinion surveys around the time of the 1983 election showed the ethnics having much the same political priorities – in believing that unemployment and defence were the most important issues – as the rest of the nation. The fascinating thing is that these issues mattered more to them than race or immigration. Thus politically, ethnics were by 1983 identifying with the population as a whole rather than with the racial minorities considered as a single group. Again, the strong support of the ethnic groups for the Labour party – surveys show two-thirds or more consistently pro-Labour – is based very little on the party's record on race issues and overwhelmingly on their perception of Labour as the party which champions the cause of the working class.[6] Thus for those who wish to marshal the racial minorities in Britain behind a programme to advance their communal interest, the prospect is not exhilarating.

Nevertheless, the perceived plight of some of the racial minority groups is an emotive issue which commands widespread sympathy. On top of that there is the thriving race relations industry, with its HQ in the Commission for Racial Equality, and its countrywide network of Community Relations Councils, units in local government, specialists installed in the educational and social services, in unions and in various institutes and charitable trusts promoting support for ethnic interests. But what impact has it made on the political parties and their policies?

At first blush it might appear that the influence of the race relations lobby on the governing party has been practically nil. In the forefront of Tory policy is its 'firm and fair' approach to immigration which, it is keen to point out, led to a reduction of immigration from the New Commonwealth and Pakistan from an average of 47,500 in the four years of preceding Labour government to 27,000 in 1985. Most recently the government cracked down on bogus tourists, family visitors and students from a number of New Commonwealth countries in order to relieve pressure on immigration officials. It followed this with penalties on airlines which were flying in people, especially Tamils from Sri Lanka, with false passports. Mrs Thatcher is frequently labelled 'racist' for her reference, just before she took office, to the danger of being 'swamped' by immigrants. She was, however, giving voice to a widespread popular feeling. Had she not done so the steam behind that feeling might have powered the engines of the National Front, which at that time was taking votes from Labour. Indeed in the seventies the front was targeting Labour areas with considerable success. In its peak year, 1977, it polled over 10 per cent in eleven Labour-held constituencies in the Greater London Council elections. What is more, 'studies of NF sympathizers have found them disproportionately in groups which have traditionally supported Labour'.[7]

Yet on race policy at home the Tories have been more influenced by the race relations lobby than one might expect. They are particularly sensitive to accusations of racial discrimination. That is doubtless why the hierarchy took a report by the Young Conservatives in 1983, about racist infiltration of the party, far more seriously than was merited by the shoddy quality of its research. Just how little the report was to be relied on was forcefully brought home to the BBC when in 1986 the corporation was sued by MPs Neil Hamilton and Gerald Howarth for libel uttered in a 'Panorama' programme, largely based on the report's findings. The BBC, after much bluster about how strong its evidence was (though much of it was shown in court to be absurdly inaccurate) eventually settled for substantial damages, which added to the even more substantial lawyers' fees, cost it half a million pounds. This débâcle had a good deal to do with the subsequent resignation of the then Director General, Alastair Milne.

Tory sensitivity about being thought to be on the wrong side of the moral divide over race has also impinged on its policy in government. As we have seen, the reaction of Home Secretary, Willie Whitelaw, to the 1981 riots was to appoint the 'liberal' judge Lord Scarman to report on them and then to accept and implement the softly-softly policing policy he recommended. The combination of that policy's apparent failure in the 1985 riots and the appointment as Home Secretary of Douglas Hurd, hailed the introduction of a sterner approach to policing. But the spirit of appeasement still lurked in Whitehall; it was given an airing by a junior minister at the Home Office, David Waddington, who in October 1985 gave an interview in which he expressed guarded support for preferential treatment for certain racial groups where they were under-represented. According to *The Times*, he was simply repeating a rather garbled version of a proposal for contract compliance put forward in a paper from the CRE, which had been on his desk since July.[8] This idea that firms should lose government contracts if they didn't employ a proportionate ratio of black and Asian staff was swiftly and angrily repudiated by junior employment minister, Alan Clark, with the backing of the new Secretary of State for Employment, Lord Young.

Curiously the same proposal was made by another junior minister in the Department of Employment, Peter Bottomley, the following month. He was also shouted down, not only by fellow Conservative MPs but by employers' organizations including the Confederation of British Industry. For contract compliance was simply not compatible with the deregulation approach which Lord Young had made his own. The idea was finally scotched by the Tory-dominated Commons Select Committee on employment which in February 1987 issued a report refusing to endorse proposals for contract compliance put forward by the Labour party and the TUC.[9]

In line with the same shift in opinion, Sir George Young, who was appointed as a junior minister in the Department of the Environment with special responsibility for ethnic minorities after the riots in 1981, was dismissed in 1986 and his department dismantled.

Why was not the same fate visited upon the Commission for Racial Equality? It is, after all, the kind of quango which Mrs Thatcher heartily dislikes. Moreover, in 1982 a countrywide discussion promoted by the Conservative Political Centre and which could be taken as representative of rank and file Tory opinion, took a majority view against positive laws on race relations and wanted to see the end of the entire race relations 'industry'.

Probably the CRE was kept simply because its abolition, especially following the riots of 1981, might be seen as too provocative. It might also have undermined the growing efforts of the Tories to strengthen links with the ethnic communities through organizations like the Anglo-West Indian and Anglo-Asian Conservative Societies, though the latter suffered from factional disputes with Sikhs which were really echoes of the troubles in the Punjab. There is also the Durbar Club, which includes well-to-do Asian businessmen among its members and which raised £75,000 for a computer to be installed in Tory Central Office. The probability is that in due course a great many Tory candidates for Parliament and for local councils will emerge from these organizations. The Conservatives' version of black sections doesn't seem to have done the party any harm.

All things considered it is unlikely that, while Mrs Thatcher stays in charge, the Tory government is going to be drawn into any of the schemes dreamed up by the race relations lobby for 'reverse discrimination'. She is fully aware of the fact that these attempts to offset injustices are in practice harmful to both blacks and whites.

It is difficult to talk of Alliance policy in the wake of the split between the pro- and anti-merger factions in the SDP following the 1987 general election. Nevertheless the 1987 Alliance manifesto may be taken as broadly representative of the parties at present headed by David Steel, Robert Maclennan and David Owen. In that, while there was plenty of robust sense about retaining immigration controls, the guiding hand on internal policy was obviously that of Roy Jenkins, who created the original Race Relations Board and set in motion the process which led to the establishment of the Commission for Racial Equality. The most important specific undertaking was 'positive steps through such measures as contract compliance, to secure equal opportunities for racial minorities'. Although the phrase 'positive discrimination' was in fact avoided, there is no doubt, following enquiries by the author, that that is what the Alliance had in mind. In any case, contract compliance is a back-door method of introducing quotas, a very positive (and damaging) form of racial discrimination indeed. The Alliance also proposed to give the CRE the power it has been tirelessly seeking, to initiate enquiries at whim without having first to refer to the Home Secretary – a power which would effectively enable the commission to harass any organization or individual at will. Such policies, which might at first glance appear to be moderate and meriting the support of all people of goodwill, might prove to be engines of oppression.

The Labour party remains the favourite of the ethnic groups. This overwhelming identification with one party might be thought to diminish the influence of the race relations lobby: one might suppose that Labour may take the ethnics' support for granted and make no effort to retain their trust. Yet this is not necessarily so: the fact of such loyalty makes the ethnic groups a potentially crucial electoral factor and therefore well worth the other parties' expending energy to win over. The Community Relations Commission underlined this point when it analysed the 1974 general elections. It showed that there were fifty-nine seats where the ethnic vote was larger than the majority of the winning candidate and that these included thirteen out of the seventeen seats won by Labour from the Conservatives to secure its majority at the second time of asking in October.[10]

For the same reason, in a period of declining fortunes, Labour has been anxious to hang on to one source of support which has remained steadfast, and has generally acceded to sectional ethnic demands. This concern was perhaps uppermost in the mind of Labour's leader, Neil Kinnock, when on a visit to India in 1985 he promised that the next Labour government would scrap the 1971 Immigration Act and the British Nationality Act of 1981 – the twin pillars of Britain's system of immigration control. In detail, he undertook to:

Ease the rules on fiancés and husbands, which would bring in 1,500 more young men per year, followed eventually by their parents.

Ease restrictions on parents, which would admit a further 500 people each year.

Give automatic rights of citizenship and residence to everybody born in Britain. This would admit children born to those staying temporarily, say as students, a measure which would add 3,000 people a year.

Allocate unclaimed immigration vouchers, amounting to 2,400 a year, to Indian applicants wishing to enter Britain. With children this might mean a further 5,000 immigrants each year.

Labour also strongly opposed the government's bill to fine airlines flying in bogus refugees without proper papers.

Of course, going by past experience of Labour in power, one is entitled to be sceptical about how long this generous policy would last, but such a specific pledge would for a while, say for two or three years, need to be translated into fact – until the next immigration crisis led to a sudden tightening up, as in 1978.

As far as their policies in Britain are concerned there has been, on Labour's part, an even more pronounced capitulation in principle to ethnic special interests. This ought to have been spelt out in the Labour manifesto for the 1987 general election, but that notoriously evasive document was in fact rather more guarded on the race issue than the Alliance manifesto. The broad (and intriguingly similar) commitment was there 'to encourage contract compliance and other positive means of continuing equity for all citizens', but the formula was vaguer – certainly vaguer than the Labour manifesto of 1983. That undertook to strengthen the Race Relations Act, to provide greatly expanded funds for ethnic minority projects, the keeping of ethnic records and a programme (in the CRE-approved phrase) of 'positive action' in employment, education, housing and social services.

The lack of specifics in the 1987 version may have been due to a realization of how unpopular inverted racism, as practised especially by 'loony left' councils up and down the country, had become. The policy of reverse discrimination practised by such local councils was in fact fully compatible with the national policies of the Labour party, but the councils had a reputation for being anti-police and revolutionary with which Labour did not wish to be identified. As Ken Livingstone put it, the GLC and councils like it had been 'into all the things she [Mrs Thatcher] didn't like – lesbian and gay rights, black people and feminism'. Examples abound, as the first chapter showed, of how this policy applied to the ethnic community, whether in the form of subsidies to black groups, or, whatever the actual words used to describe it, the practice of reverse discrimination in employment, housing and education. The approach was distilled in the parting words of Mrs Frances Morell, when a surprise vote by her colleagues on the Inner London Education Authority dismissed her from its leadership. She complained that a 'white middle-class man' had succeeded her, whereas she had 'wanted the revolution to continue'. Such a remark would seem to indicate a policy of seeking to create a coalition of all the discontented minorities in the belief that together they would form a majority. This is a dubious enough proposition even in local government, where the election turnout is low; at a national level it is an impossible one.

The emergence of blacks from Labour's ranks to become councillors and parliamentary candidates for winnable and safe seats should have been cause for self-congratulation among the party leadership – yet the radical stance of most of these politicians is likely to reduce Labour's chances of being re-elected to government yet further. Mention has already been made of Bernie Grant, the council leader in the London borough of Haringey and recently elected Member of Parliament, who may never live down his comment on the Tottenham riots that the police got 'a bloody good hiding'. Diane Abbott, newly elected Labour Member for Hackney North and Britain's first black woman MP, provided ammunition for Tory party chairman Norman Tebbit by having been co-writer of the following: 'We are not interested in reforming the prevailing institutions – of the police, armed services, judiciary and monarchy – through which the ruling class keep us in "our" place. We are about dismantling them and replacing them with our own machinery of class rule.'[11]

In Brent South the Labour member is Paul Boateng, a lawyer who became a folk hero in certain quarters for defending alleged rioters. He was also chairman of the police committee of the Greater London Council which spent £200,000 a year on 'research' but was actually a vehicle for attacking the Metropolitan Police whom he once described as 'riddled with racists'.

Not a parliamentary candidate but occupying an equally high-profile position as successor to 'Red' Ted Grant is the leader of Lambeth council, Linda Bellos, who has frequently attacked the Labour leadership over its policy towards blacks.

These and others like them arose from the black sections of the

Labour party, which had their first annual conference in Birmingham in June 1984 with an attendance of 300, despite the frosty disapproval of the leadership. A campaign was launched, backed by leading left-wing MPs Tony Benn and Eric Heffer, for official recognition by the Labour party and the right to guaranteed representation in the upper councils of the party. It was argued that in principle there was no difference between black sections and those already established for women and youth. Neil Kinnock, however, took a different view and led a vote of Labour's National Executive in July 1985 to reject the black sections proposal by fifteen votes to seven.

Kinnock condemned the whole idea as party 'apartheid'.[12] He was naturally concerned to avoid giving official approval to another extremist organization – Labour had had enough trouble with Trotskyites of the Militant Tendency in its youth section. Besides, Labour's standard reply to those who sought to identify the party with its radical left was that the radical left was confined to a handful of fringe politicians in a few inner-city boroughs; if black sections were established this would provide the extremists with platforms to propagate their views right across the land. He was probably concerned too about the likelihood of alienating traditional white working-class support for Labour by any arrangement which would seem to give special privileges within the party to blacks.

Despite the National Executive's opposition, the black sections, with left-wing support, continued to function unofficially. At Lewisham East in London the selection of a prospective parliamentary candidate by a committee on which black sections were represented was declared void and the local party told to re-select. There was talk of those blacks who entered Parliament as Labour MPs forming a black caucus in the House of Commons.[13] As the general election drew nearer the party leaders became increasingly worried about the conduct of these unofficial black sections and the damage they were doing to the party's image. In March 1987, the fourth annual conference of the unrecognized black sections[14] was called at Nottingham with a paper for debate which attacked police 'atrocities' and called for elected authority control over police operations day-to-day. The conference was not open to white journalists.[15] A black sections meeting held the following month in Birmingham, the home territory of deputy Labour leader

134

Roy Hattersley and showpiece of moderate socialism, really set off the alarm. Prospective Labour parliamentary candidates were warned not to attend on pain of losing the official party nomination. One black activist who was Labour's choice for Nottingham East, however, did attend. This was Sharon Atkin, a former Lambeth councillor who had been disqualified for breaking the rate-capping laws. At Birmingham in front of a red banner decorated with a clenched-fist salute reminiscent of the Black Power movement of the 1960s, Sharon Atkin declared: 'I don't give a damn about Neil Kinnock and a racist Labour party.'[16] This conference also produced a ten-point 'secret' black manifesto proposing to:

1. Spend millions of pounds of public money on creating jobs for blacks in inner cities.

2. Open up civil-service and town-hall jobs by lowering entry standards for blacks while demanding higher qualifications from whites.

3. Appoint black activists to top posts in the supposedly politically neutral civil service.

4. Set up police watchdog committees to monitor the force while 'looking after the interests of black youths'.

5. Scrap immigration controls.

6. Halt all trade with South Africa and bar South African citizens from Britain.

7. Forge links with Cuba and other hard-left anti-American states.

8. Name national monuments and beauty spots after African revolutionaries – Dartmoor, for example, becoming Mangaliso Sobukwe National Park.

9. Form a black MPs caucus who would vote together in Parliament.

10. Engineer activist candidates into safe seats to ensure a larger proportion of black MPs.

It was the defiance of Ms Atkin, however, and her application to the Labour party of the ritual insult 'racist' that enraged the Labour leaders. By suspending her parliamentary candidacy they took their revenge. Linda Bellos then appeared on BBC radio and also called the Labour party 'racist' but nobody seemed to admonish her. In any case, if the criterion for sacking Ms Atkin was bringing discredit on the party why, it must be asked, hadn't Bernie Grant been dismissed much earlier for his remarks about the police? The answer is surely that, as in the case of the Liverpool Militants, this was tokenism, the public slaying of a puffed-up dragon to demonstrate to the press and media that the Labour leadership were not prepared to tolerate extremism. The reality was and remains different. The black sections are still active in the Labour party and unlikely to change their ways.

Nevertheless this whole performance underlines the short-sightedness of the black leadership. As Paul Johnson commented at the time: 'In the whole of British history it is hard to think of any minority community which has been so badly led. If the black leaders had deliberately set out to antagonize the rest of the nation they could not have done it more effectively.'[17] Black political activism is self-defeating because it stresses the separateness of the blacks instead of their identity with the rest of British community life. We have yet to see the full consequences of the extra-ordinarily foolish attempt of a few leading blacks to hijack the Labour party and use it as a vehicle for extorting preferential treatment for ethnic minority groups.

9

Anti-Racism versus Freedom

In the demonology of the 'anti-racists' lobby blacks are poor and humiliated largely because of exploitation by whites. The cry of 'race equality' is therefore at least in part a demand for economic and social justice. It might be said that the anti-racist movement has applied a Marxist analysis of economics to the sphere of race relations, with whites in the role of capitalists and blacks as the working class. The parallel should warn us that simple appeals to our sense of justice, from 'anti-racists' as from Marxists, may mask sinister and subversive aims.

In practice the demand that the racial minorities shall have a juster distribution of status and rewards means replacing the free contractual arrangements between individuals by various forms of coercion by the state. When Communists take over a formerly free country they substitute the inequality of political and bureaucratic status – with all the control over the use of material resources that that implies – for simple inequality of wealth. Similarly many 'anti-racists' seek to impose a type of inequality which would give themselves more power, putting within their gift jobs, housing, special treatment by the welfare services, even the bestowing of qualifications through the grading of examinations and tests now controlled by others. The requirement that in almost every kind of transaction the ethnics must be fairly treated would result in the creation or enhancement in status of a huge number of posts of race controllers, supervisors, advisers, investigators, assessors, arbitrators, prosecutors and judges, not to mention police. Clearly this would limit the freedom of the majority, and it is doubtful that there would be any compensating growth of freedom or even material gain for the ethnic minorities who are supposed to be the beneficiaries of such change. They may have special provision made for them where they had none before, but the price may be a new servitude to those who dispose of such privilege. All dependence means some freedom denied.

There is the subsidiary point that by being politicized ethnics may shy away from economically productive work. It may become easier to acquire an income or obtain a lucrative position through being on good terms with a politician or an official than to qualify for it by working hard. This will both demoralize and impoverish people while also making them less independent. This argument is not academic. There are many parts of the world, including large parts of Africa and South America, where the social and political system is so debased that people who spend their days in useful toil are vastly worse off than those who constantly butter up, bribe and 'keep in with' corrupt politicians and officials. It is a social order which Professor Andreski has christened 'kleptocracy',[1] or organized robbery which starts at the top. The outstanding characteristic of all countries run on this basis is that, however rich they may be in natural resources, their peoples are wretchedly poor.

The most obvious form which anti-racism regulation takes is interference with freedom of contract. A good example is the imposition of a statutory minimum wage which prevents the fixing of a wage below that figure even if it is voluntarily agreed between employer and employee. As has been mentioned in the chapter on American experience, in those states which imposed minimum wage rates the level of black youth unemployment jumped from being the same as for white youth to around twice as high. For the blacks who were thus put out of work the inability to take a job at a lower wage than the minimum rate was a real deprivation. A statutory minimum wage would rob many Asian married women in Britain who do piecework at home, where they are tied by custom and by young children, of what are sometimes described as 'starvation' wages, but which are still better than the alternative of nothing at all. Often these earnings are crucial in providing the savings which create a family business and the independence which goes with it. To be in favour of a minimum wage, as Britain's Labour party currently is, may sound like being on the side of the poorest, most downtrodden workers. Yet governments in South

Africa intent on preserving apartheid deliberately used minimum wage laws to that end. Their aim was to reserve most jobs in certain occupations for whites. When they used quotas there was a temptation for employers to use more of the cheaper black labour than they were allowed. But after the imposition of minimum wage laws employers were reluctant to hire blacks at the same wage as whites.

Unions, again, are supposed to be the workers' champions but they actually have a corporate monopoly interest in stopping the employment of workers below union rates. It is thus no coincidence that the Low Pay Unit, which constantly issues pamphlets deploring such practices as the use of sweated labour and has campaigned for the preservation of the wages councils (which impose wage minima on three million workers and which the Tories at one time threatened to abolish), is substantially dependent on trade unions for its funds. Not surprisingly the Labour party, which also receives 95 per cent of its funds from trade unions, is also committed to the introduction of a statutory minimum wage.

It is true that the Labour party (like the Alliance) declares itself to be against racial discrimination in employment and in favour of 'positive action'. It may thus be able to counter the detrimental effects to the ethnic minorities of a minimum wage. But imposing quotas or percentages of ethnic minority workers which organizations and firms must maintain nearly always involves lowering the standards which need to be achieved in order to qualify for a job. An unintended effect of this is to undermine the status of ethnics who qualify because people naturally assume that their qualification must be below par for the majority. Recently a black New York policeman refused to accept promotion to sergeant because, though he had passed the necessary examination and attained the marks required for ethnic minority candidates he had not reached the level demanded of the whites. He said he didn't want to be a 'quota sergeant'. He must have spoken for many self-respecting blacks who feel demeaned and their striving and achievements devalued by protection of this kind.

In many organizations the Commission for Racial Equality has found a back-door method of introducing what amount to ethnic quotas. Its method is to call on employers to monitor how many ethnic minority employees they have on their books. The proportion of ethnics to the total staff is then compared with the proportion of ethnics in the local population. If the ratio in the firm is lower the ethnics are said to be under-represented.

This is a deliberate confusion of equality of opportunity with equality of result. There is not the slightest reason to suppose that the lack of correspondence between the two percentages indicates racial discrimination; there are many other factors at work. All the same the CRE has managed to impose this *non sequitur* on a host of government and local government bodies and about a hundred large private firms, including the clearing banks.[2]

The idea of imposing racial quotas has been strongly advocated by John Carr in a Fabian pamphlet published in January 1987.[3] The form which this particular proposal takes is the relatively new one of contract compliance. This is the policy of requiring those who receive public contracts to use a certain ratio of ethnic workers in carrying it out. It is copied from the USA where it is claimed that it has had a great success. Yet it is open to the same objections as a straightforward quota system, which, indirectly, is exactly what it is. Keeping up the ratio invariably involves lowering qualification standards, implying that ethnics are not sufficiently competent to pass at the same level as whites. It encourages us to ignore better solutions to the problem and is frequently harmful to the ethnics themselves.[4] It also implies large-scale resort to regulation at a time when governments are beginning to realize what damage to the economy regulations usually inflict.

A variant on the basic principle of positive action, though applied negatively, is the suspension from certain occupations or activities of people who are accused of racist conduct. Such is the effect of the Black List operated by the United Nations Special Committee Against Apartheid. Dozens of top British sporting personalities have been excluded from competing in certain countries, including Nick Faldo, Harvey Smith and Sir Stanley Matthews. Their 'offence' has been to take part in sporting events in South Africa, by which action they are judged to support apartheid. Yet the underlying assumption of this measure – that anybody involved in South African sport is an accomplice in that country's racial policy – is surely highly questionable. The British government is in an equivocal position on sporting sanctions, having signed the Gleneagles Agreement by which it has undertaken to discourage sporting links with South Africa. Yet it has consistently opposed other forms of sanction. Its other mistake was to have appointed a minister of sport, because this makes politicians overseas assume that sport is a political matter in Britain – a collectivist idea with which Conservatives at least should have nothing to do. For it belongs to the totalitarian way of thinking according to which everything in human affairs lies within the province of politics. The civilized idea, which has taken such a beating in this century, is that sport, like art, music, entertainment, religion, romantic love and family life, belongs to the civic culture which does not serve political ends.

The United Nations Black List extends to entertainment as well as sport, with more than 200 international showbusiness personalities appearing on it. British stars on the list have included Cliff Richard, Shirley Bassey and Spike Milligan.[5] Moreover, in April 1986 the British actors' union, Equity, voted to ban its members from visiting South Africa under pain of expulsion. This was not a penalty to take lightly because, in this tightly organized and unionized profession, the loss of their union card means for most members the end of their career. The Equity ban came as a result of a postal ballot on a motion of the leftists in the union, in which just over 10 per cent took part and for which even so there was only a 58 per cent majority vote. Derek Bond, Equity president and former star of the West End farce, *No Sex Please, We're British*, resigned and Janet Suzman, a multi-prize-winning South African-born actress, was furious like many others at this gratuitous union interference with its members' affairs. She said, 'This ban is a lousy, stupid idea. No union has a right to dictate what a person's conscience should be. I abhor apartheid – but I also abhor political censorship. And politics should not come into any artistic profession.'[6] It was ironic that, in order to register a protest against (among other aspects of apartheid) the South African pass laws – which dictate where people may work and live – the activists of Equity were seeking to impose pass laws on their own members. Happily a case was brought against the union and a High Court judge found that they were exceeding their authority – a true victory for civil liberty.

Yet more worrying than these attempts to influence people's behaviour by restricting their freedom to perform wherever they like, is the bid to win control of people's intellectual development.

The anti-racist lobby fully realizes that the most effective way to impose its ideas on the population is to make them part of everybody's mental furniture. It can attempt to do this by building such ideas into the nation's education system, prescribing how it is to be organized and what is to be taught. This is what the Swann Report, already referred to, apparently set out to do. As we have seen that report failed to answer the question of why West Indian children on average performed badly in school. The reason for that failure was that the committee made the fallacious assumption that equality of opportunity should mean equality of result. The inequality of West Indian academic performance could therefore only reflect unequal opportunities of which racialism must be the cause. Faced with a perceived failure of West Indians to adapt to British ways, as their poor school performance indicated, the Swann Report's prescription was that British society should be changed to accommodate West Indians, and other ethnic groups. This was to be done by conditioning the teachers in racial awareness courses and transforming the curriculum by placing far less emphasis upon English language and culture. The specific proposals which deserve attention (some were toned down in the final report but this is the general gist) were:

- an end to morning assembly with prayers;
- the teaching of ethnic group languages such as Gujerati, Punjabi and Creole even in all-white schools;
- the teaching of other subjects in these languages;
- the material taught in all subjects to be in accordance with the values of a multi-racial society and to the detriment of British patriotic pride;
- Ethnocentrism – in this case a European view of the world – to be expunged in the teaching of history and immigration to be presented as the legacy of the allegedly shameful episodes of empire and slavery.[7]

Such is the influence of the anti-racist establishment and its minions that this report, instead of being summarily rejected, was received seriously when it came out and many educational authorities, with the egregious Inner London Education to the fore, treated it as a *vade mecum*. Woe betide anyone in the education industry who dared to criticize the philosophy which it evidently distilled even before its final, as opposed to its interim, conclusions appeared. Yet one bold spirit, Ray Honeyford, headmaster of Drummond Middle School in Bradford, where 90 per cent of the pupils were Asian or black, did so dare in the winter of 1984. Writing in the obscure but academically eminent *Salisbury Review*, he accused the race lobby of exploiting the tolerance traditional in this country in order to induce and maintain feelings of guilt in the well-disposed majority, so that 'decent' people are 'not only afraid of voicing certain thoughts, they are uncertain even of their right to think those thoughts'. He criticized the dishonest terminology foisted on people by the race lobby. For instance there was the the word 'racism' itself, which he called 'a slogan designed to suppress constructive thought . . . the icon word of those committed to the race game'. He also objected to the perversion of the word 'black' to mean all non-whites with the obvious purpose of creating an atmosphere of anti-white solidarity. This was the preliminary before launching into specific complaints. He deplored the practice of many Asian parents of sending their children back to their homeland for a holiday during term-time to the detriment of their education. He objected strongly to the way they regarded freedom to do so contrary to law as a right. He also drew attention to the unrecognized plight of the white working-class children whose education was suffering in schools where they were hopelessly outnumbered by children from ethnic groups. He went on to reject the claim that West Indian educational failure owed anything to teacher prejudice or an alien curriculum and attributed it instead to 'West Indian family structure and values and the work of misguided radical teachers whose motives are basically political'. He finished by listing the various elements which were gathered together under the banner of multi-racialism and expressed his view that, far from producing harmony, they were operating to produce 'a sense of fragmentation and discord'.

These comments produced an explosion of wrath and mendacious propaganda from local activists of the race lobby who tried to have Mr Honeyford dismissed and, by constant abuse and picketing of the school, sought to make his life a misery. The Bradford Education Authority suspended him and though he was reinstated after a prolonged battle in the courts he eventually settled regretfully for early retirement, though on quite generous terms.

Jonathan Savery, who worked for the Local Education Authority in Avon which supported Mr Honeyford, also wrote in the *Salisbury Review*. As a result he was not only suspended by his employer but set upon by his colleagues. The National Union of Teachers, which had rightly shown itself anxious to defend Miss Maureen McGoldrick against Brent council's fabricated charges, instructed its members not to work with Mr Savery because he was a 'racist'. Which, as the *Salisbury Review* editorial was quick to observe, showed that merely to be charged with 'racism' nowadays is sufficient to be presumed guilty.

There is also some reason for thinking that the truth about events where a racial element is involved is being withheld. As was pointed out in Chapter Seven, the Metropolitan Police published figures in March 1983 on muggings in London which showed that over half of them were committed by blacks. Yet, though this information is of public interest, no more figures have been produced since that date. Why? The short answer may be that, given the controversy over the figures caused by the race lobby, it is too troublesome to publish them. Such statistics are liable to complaints not only from the race relations quangos but from a militant clique in the National Union of Journalists. The NUJ code of conduct in clause 10 states, 'A journalist shall not originate material which encourages discrimination on grounds of race, colour, creed, gender or sexual orientation.' This for a start is objectionable because it is so ambiguous: no journalist can know for certain whether his or her material will encourage discrimination on grounds of race or any other of the grounds listed. Moreover the NUJ issues race relations guidelines urging members not to mention someone's race or nationality unless strictly relevant. On the face of it that sounds reasonable, but in any particular case judging what is relevant can be very difficult. The inevitable suspicion lurks that what we really have here is not a plea for fair play but for affirmative action on behalf of the racial minorities: they must always be given the benefit of the doubt. But the journalist has no business giving anybody the benefit of any doubt. His or her job is to report or establish the facts.

The guidelines also urge journalists to resist the temptation to sensationalize issues which could harm race relations. No one could object to the overt intention of that, but opinions vary about what constitutes sensationalism, and indeed about whether or not

144

there are times and issues when sensationalism is justified. The pamphlet produced by NUJ activists in conjunction with the Campaign Against Racism in the Media, *It ain't Half Racist, Mum*, has an article by Carl Gardner which outlines a plan of action for fighting racism in the printed media. It starts mildly enough, suggesting, though without conviction, writing to the editor of the newspaper concerned. It goes on to recommend a series of escalations, complaining to the Press Council, raising the matter at a staff union meeting of the newspaper, drawing in the pressure groups and the other unions, calling a public meeting, and then proceeds to direct action, with picketing and occupation of newspaper offices to demand the right of reply. With the weakening of the unions since the Thatcher union reforms these bullyboy tactics are now less feasible, but they would be back in full vigour if Labour returned to power.

Meanwhile the main 'anti-racist' pressure on newspapers comes from the Press Council, the body which was established to overlook the press in order to maintain standards. It is a necessary but unenviable job but the council has made that job more difficult by impaling itself on the NUJ rubric that reports should not include 'irrelevant' references to race or colour. For all too often the charge of irrelevance appears to be no more than an attempt at censorship. For instance in 1985 all national newspapers reported the trial of a youth who raped five women and hacked another to death with a broken milk bottle. Several mentioned that the youth was black and were condemned by the Press Council because in its view the colour of the youth was not 'relevant'. The newspapers rightly castigated the Press Council's intervention as interference with editorial prerogative.

The race lobby is also making strenuous efforts to exert control over the reporting and commenting on racial matters on television. The Commission for Racial Equality produced a special report on 'Television in a Multi-Racial Society'.[8] This yielded a series of proposals – monitoring programmes, providing more jobs for ethnics as programme-makers and actors through positive action and so on. It reads as a programme for fair treatment – but stakes out a claim to power which if realized could result in television becoming subject to authoritarian controls.

In book publishing the 'anti-racists' have been active for some time. As early as 1972 an organization called 'Teachers Against

Racism' wrote to the publisher of the famous children's classic *Little Black Sambo*, saying: 'the underlying message [of the book] is made all the more sinister by the appearance of innocence and charm. The reader swallows wholesale a totally patronizing attitude to black people who are shown as greedy [Black Sambo eats 169 pancakes], stereotyped, happy, clownish, irresponsible plantation "niggers".' This sort of pressure may well have had a cumulative effect as the book was recently reported to be out of print.[9]

There are many more examples (others have been quoted in earlier chapters). The London borough of Brent figures prominently among them. In June 1982 it was reported that, following the appointment of an adviser on multi-cultural education there, Mrs Hettie Reith, headmistress of North View Primary School, Neasden, had been examining the books in the school library for material that was racially offensive. She lit upon *Dip the Puppy* by Spike Milligan, and wrote to him complaining, 'Your book shows a character "King Blackbottom" [described in the book as a big fat man in a grass skirt and a tin top hat] which in our opinion is an example of racial stereotyping totally at variance with current attitudes.' Shortly after this complaint the Inner London Education Authority drew up a blacklist of books which were 'potentially dangerous to young minds'. It included *Dr Dolittle*, in part of which a black man is depicted as a big buffoon, and *Beau and the Beast*, in which the beast is brown. Enid Blyton was also banned for a story about a grandmother's attitude to a black family who moved in next door. One of Walter de la Mare's short stories about a black boy who took medicine to turn himself white was also considered very harmful.[10]

Back in 1978 the veteran *Times* columnist Bernard Levin revealed anti-racist feeling among librarians, normally the most civilized and genteel of folk. He found a letter in the journal *Assistant Librarian* which declared not only that librarians had a duty 'to censor all material which is racist' but called for 'violent opposition' to stop racists voicing their views in the streets. He also unearthed an organization called 'Librarians for Social Change'. One of their manifestoes pronounced: 'LFSC is a forum for the reappraisal of getting information to the people. Our members are active in fighting the isms – capitalism, fascism, racism, sexism' – but not, apparently, Communism. Yet another organization called

'Librarians against Racism and Fascism' made the following ringing declaration:

> We, as library workers, agree that it is a major function of librarianship actively to combat racism and fascism and we advocate the following: that stock selection for libraries should be guided by anti-racist and anti-fascist principles. That staff recruitment should reflect a similar policy. That local authority buildings should not be used for racist or fascist organizations.[11]

Since then there have been several cases of these reference-room activists practising what they preach. The chief librarian of the London borough of Lambeth refused to obtain for one citizen a book on the British empire, *Noon Day Sun* by Valerie Pakenham, actually an amusing and mildly satirical book on the doings amid palm and pine of the Edwardian upper classes. His objection was that it was imperialistic and did not reflect the views of the coloured South African people. Predictably Lambeth also banned *Little Black Sambo* and *Uncle Tom's Cabin*.[12]

The ideologues of the race lobby, then, are capable of exerting limited control over people's lives in many different ways. While the Tories remain in office, however, their extremer tendencies are likely to remain subject to some measure of restraint. The opposition parties, though, are committed to a forward policy on race, the details of which would almost certainly be dictated by 'experts' supplied by the race lobby. That would surely mean accepting the CRE's proposals, already referred to, for augmenting its own powers under the 1976 Race Relations Act. Such an extension of its authority would not matter so much if it were merely an attempt to appropriate the already marked-out territory of a rival bureaucracy or quangocracy. Unfortunately it would mean the acquisition by the CRE of alarming new inquisitorial and prosecutorial powers over the whole British population. Its proposals would disastrously enshrine in statute the fallacy according to which inequality of opportunity is proved by inequality of results. It would make the mere existence of 'unrepresentative' ratios of ethnic employment in any organization an automatic infraction of the law. Failure to fulfil racial quotas, which it would itself define, would become grounds for prosecution and, contrary to the whole tradition of British law, the onus of proof of innocence would rest upon the accused. And this greatly strengthened race relations law would apply far more comprehensively than it does today; for it would be given overriding priority, a great many present exemptions being elbowed out. The CRE would supervise control of immigration and 'all areas of governmental and regulatory activity' including planning control, the prisons and the police. It could also, regardless of what the Secretary of State for Education might feel, interfere in the administration of schools.

Most ominously, under the proposed new regime race relations law would be shifted out of the ordinary courts and put under a new quango within the general framework of the industrial tribunal system. This body would be able to require the payment by offenders of large and, as far as employment matters were concerned, unlimited compensation to 'victims'.

On top of that the CRE would have unrestrained powers to impose codes of conduct on any organization with regard not only to employment but to any field of human relations. Again, where employment or housing benefit was concerned it would be able with the agreement of the Secretary of State for Employment to prescribe the keeping of ethnic records and the making of returns.

If these proposals became law, the powers of the CRE to investigate and prosecute would resemble those of the Spanish Inquisition. Like Marx when he wrote the Communist manifesto, the Commission for Racial Equality scorns to conceal its intentions and no one can say that it has failed to give fair warning of what it is trying to achieve. It is entirely fitted to be the champion of the race lobby because it is so representative of so much of it, both in its hostility to our free institutions and in its urge to dismantle them in pursuit of its goal.

10

Race Harmony in a Free Society

I have argued in the preceding pages that racism is less of a problem in Britain than the extravagant response to it known as anti-racism, which has become a veritable mania. An industry of race inspectors, advisers and specialists has insinuated itself into every part of our national life. Where they have had power, as in some of our schools, they have used it dictatorially, as the persecution of Ray Honeyford in Bradford and many others less publicized has shown. This network of officials (most of them on the public payroll, but also making inroads in the private sector), has, far from furthering racial harmony which is supposed to be its purpose, fostered resentment and promoted strife.

Inevitably the race relations industry attracts some people who regard racial conflict as a means by which this country's democratic institutions may be undermined. For them the ethnic minorities are pawns in a class war whose divisions are drawn by race.

Yet the offensive against racism could not be sustained did it not touch deep chords in the national psyche relating to traumatic episodes in Britain's past. The word 'racism' arouses strong feelings because it evokes thoughts of Hitler, the British Empire and immigration. A combination of horror and misplaced sense of guilt shaped the liberal approach to racial issues in the post-war period. As a result it was easy for the anti-racist lobby to establish itself and become dominant in British life.

So it is that we are still contending with the quango legacy of politicians of 'liberal' cast of mind, the most conspicuous of whom was Roy Jenkins, Home Secretary in the critical mid-sixties. His view – that immigration was good for Britain and that the majority should be socially engineered into accepting it – dictated our race relations legislation. It is he who is primarily responsible for the shift of emphasis from a limited semi-judicial function, dealing with acts of overt racial discrimination in public places and incitement to racial hatred, into active widespread harassment of organizations and individuals and the spreading of activist propaganda.

It did not take long for what eventually became the Commission for Racial Equality to follow the familiar path of regulative quangos and get taken over by a pressure group, in this case to become a mouthpiece of the ethnic groups. This partisanship of course conflicted with the CRE's judicial role. In any case the results of Jenkins's innovations were not happy in either sphere. Court cases bringing ordinary people to the dock over advertisements for Scottish cooks, Italian singers and European girlfriends, made the board, as it then was, a laughing-stock. There were many complaints about firms being investigated and arraigned to no good purpose and at great expense. The propaganda directed at the ethnic groups was even worse, being generally negative and inclined to encourage a dependency and a readiness to excuse every failing by blaming it on racial bias. Yet despite its poor results and signal lack of ordinary competence, which was underlined by a House of Commons Select Committee in 1981, the CRE harbours extraordinary ambitions for the extension of its role. In particular it seeks powers to enforce, throughout the length and breadth of the economy, policies of reverse discrimination or affirmative action which would create a bureaucratic nightmare and put valued traditional freedoms under threat. But these policies have already been tried and found wanting in the United States. The anti-poverty programme of President Lyndon Johnson and his successors has been disastrous. At a cost so huge that it undermined the standing of the American dollar it has succeeded only in making the situation of the poor blacks worse. This criticism has been eloquently voiced by a number of distinguished black academics of various disciplines. In CRE circles, though, indeed in the race relations industry as a whole, they and economists such as Thomas Sowell seem to be either unknown or wilfully ignored. Nor do the CRE bureaucrats seem to be aware of Charles Murray's path-breaking *Losing Ground* which shows up the fundamental defects of the anti-poverty programme: its stress on rights instead of duties, its emphasis on state (federal) assistance instead of neighbourhood help and the paternalism which robs the poor of freedom and dignity of choice.

The spectacular riots of 1981 in Brixton, Birmingham and Liverpool led to the official enquiry by the liberal-minded Lord Scarman. In essence it traced the disturbances to two common causes – police brutality and deprivation. The recommendations led to the adoption of a softly-softly approach to policing in racially-sensitive areas. The diagnosis was flawed and its prescription counter-productive. Many of the police felt that it led ineluctably to the failure at an early stage to control the 1985 Tottenham riot in which PC Blakelock was killed.

Certainly the softly-softly policy did not stimulate any corresponding softening on the part of the race-lobby activists who in this period seemed more eager than ever to vilify the police. The Scarman Report became a standard progressive text, less for its philosophy of policing than for its pronouncement that the riots were caused by underlying social conditions such as joblessness, bad housing and poverty's inevitable toll. The standard progressive answer to this problem was to increase public spending in these areas. Yet there had to be doubts about such a solution if only because the riot areas had received more than most in the form of government grants. Moreover, the evidence did not support the contention that the ethnics were a deprived underclass. In particular the Asians who constituted half the ethnic population were in many respects, such as house ownership, educational achievement and business enterprise, doing remarkably well. The core of the inner-city problem, in so far as it was an ethnic one, was that of the West Indians. They suffered more from planning and municipal socialism than other inner-city dwellers because of their weak family structure, which was notable for the disproportionate number of one-parent, meaning in practice fatherless, families.

In many of Britain's inner cities comprehensive development planning has bought out and removed the small businesses and property-owners. This has not only destroyed a great many jobs but taken away such areas' natural leaders, leaving behind communities lacking in internal discipline, easy prey to crime, vandalism and drugs. Municipal socialism, with its high rates, has

151

driven away yet more businesses large and small, and encouraged the building of monster high-rise blocks of flats which are breeding grounds of social disorder and crime. All that the race relations industry and the left have to offer the West Indians caught in this trap are aggressive cultural chauvinism and welfare dependency which will inevitably make their condition worse.

Those who persuade the ethnic communities that racial discrimination is the source of their ills and that politics is the cure are misleading them. As Lord Scarman said, there is no institutional racism in Britain and, unlike the American blacks, our ethnic minorities do not have to campaign for civil rights which they have long enjoyed. Politicians who offer to improve their condition by passing laws to end discrimination are in fact advocating special treatment. The terrible plight of the North American Indians, who probably have more government-provided racial privilege than any other racial minority group in the world, is a warning to our ethnics to beware of those who, like the Greeks, come bearing gifts.

The good news is that neither the blacks nor the other ethnic minorities seem attracted to the communal approach to politics, but are swayed in their voting by national issues like unemployment rather than specifically ethnic issues such as racial discrimination. That is a good sign because Britain's blacks will prosper if they absorb themselves, as other ethnic groups have done, into the mainstream of British national life.

The laws and policies advocated by the race lobby to combat racism would not only do nothing to improve the material condition of the ethnic minorities but would also gravely infringe the traditional liberties of one and all. The harassment of numerous teachers and headmasters by left-wing local authorities is a pointer to the kind of tyranny that would be practised on a much larger scale. Even under the government of Mrs Thatcher the censoring influence of the race lobby on newspapers and the media through the Press Council, the TV and Radio Broadcasting Council and the activists of the National Union of Journalists has been worrying, as has the censoring at local level of books and nursery rhymes.

It would not of course be practical to legislate against such perverse anti-racism, but there is certainly no reason to go on allowing public funds to sustain it. On the contrary, much would be gained by dismantling its infrastructure. It would be tempting from this point of view to abolish the Commission for Racial Equality altogether as well as the race relations legislation through which it came to be. Yet on balance there is a better case for reverting to the modest ambitions of the 1965 Act. These were to prevent incitement to racial hatred by making it a criminal offence, and to shield ethnic minorities against wounding overt acts of discrimination in public places. Incitement is a straightforward matter which should be dealt with by the police. Discrimination in public places should where necessary be dealt with by injunction obtained by the Attorney-General, but preferably through the conciliation of the (as it then was) Race Relations Board. Admittedly this arrangement would leave *in situ* a band of race relations officers intent on exposing contraventions of the law. Yet it does address the problem of real racist behaviour which creates greater race tensions, generates ill-will among racial minorities and may lead to breaches of the peace. All the rest of the CRE apparatus, including its investigative, informative and propagandist functions should disappear.

Repealing the 1968 legislation, then, would not only dispense with most of the general staff of the race relations army but would also drastically reduce the race relations personnel in many private organizations and firms. Admittedly, at the local government level, where most of the race relations officers would not be needed either, they would probably be retained on ideological grounds. However, their influence should be limited by the change in the law, by the government's proposed reorganization of local government and by its programme for the inner cities. Laws are in train to limit the scope of local council spending on political objectives. Where legislation fails to reduce extravagance and bad management the reform of the rates to create an incentive towards economy in local government should do better; extraneous posts like those of race relations officers appointed to enforce legislation which has been repealed should be cancelled. In the inner cities left-wing councils and planning officials will be required to let private contractors bid for a host of services like street cleaning, refuse collection and catering and will be bypassed if they do not co-operate. In this way a sizeable economy may be de-municipalized and opportunities created for local firms.

But how will the ethnic minorities fare under these arrangements? Few doubt that the Asians will flourish. They have become kings of the corner shop; indeed they probably saved the corner shop from extinction just as it came under the supermarkets' competitive threat. Godfrey Smith, writing in *The Sunday Times*,[1] referred to Maheed Mohammed, a Kashmiri Muslim, who would certainly welcome such changes. He complained that Brent council was forcing him to shut his supermarket next to Willesden tube station at 8.00 p.m. instead of midnight as was his wont, forcing him to work ninety hours a week instead of 110. As Smith observed, 'The Asians have found, with astonishing ease, yawning gaps in the British economy where it looks almost laughably easy to make money – provided you work hard enough and long enough.'

There are at least 400 Asian millionaires (of whom 100 or more are called Patel). The Durbar Club of Asian businessmen, referred to earlier, which supports the Conservative party, has an annual subscription of £1,000. Most of its members have prospered not only through their own hard work, but because their whole family works as well; they don't take wages, so minimum wage laws don't affect them, and they plough their profits back into the business. It is characteristic of the anti-business psychology of many of our academics that a study by four Liverpool Polytechnic lecturers of Asian shops in 1982 decided that they were doomed. It concluded that their system, requiring long anti-social hours of work from the owner and substantial unpaid work from his family, was a waste of capital, talent and energy. The Asian shopkeepers remind one of the bee which the scientists, on the basis of aerodynamic theory, proved could not fly. The bee, unburdened by any knowledge of aerodynamics, just carries on flying.

But what about the West Indians? Certainly they have been conspicuously successful in sport. The Afro-Caribbean contribution to British sport is now phenomenal. Their one per cent of the population provided a third of Britain's team to the Los Angeles Olympics. They dominate boxing. It is predicted that half the players in professional football by the end of this decade will be black. The skill of West Indian cricketers is legendary. Certainly in sport the test – winning a race, or jumping higher or further than others or scoring more goals – is objective and race prejudice cannot affect the outcome. Yet perhaps it is more significant that sport is an area of life where the Afro-Caribbeans have confidence that they can win. Role models like Daley Thompson and Tessa Sanderson have bred a host of imitators among black youth, all reaching for the stars. Black performers have provided heroes for whites too and this has done more to counter racial prejudice than anything the race relations lobby has ever done. Typically the CRE has tended to ignore black success in sport and has drawn attention to occasions when crowds boo black players in order to show that race prejudice is on the increase. Yet it is a matter of record that in the USA black athletic prowess did more than anything else to breach the racial barriers in the universities of the Deep South. Nationally the brilliance of black players at baseball and basketball has done infinitely more for racial integration than any number of laws.

The justified hope is that the confidence engendered by black success in sport is spilling over into other areas of life. The effort and self-discipline through which Daley Thompson became the world decathlon champion would take a man to the top in any walk of life. He himself said, 'Even though all the other kids in school were white I never sensed I was different at all.' He believes that blackness is only an obstacle if it is allowed to be. 'If I went for a job where two A-levels were needed and a white guy with one A-level got the job, then I'd go away and get a university degree, then go back for the same job . . . I wouldn't even allow myself to think that colour had entered into it.'[2]

The West Indians do not have the merchanting tradition of the Asians or the kinds of families which work together as a unit without any individual wages. Yet something is moving. As mentioned earlier, West Indians are more motivated than the majority of whites and stay at school longer. When John MacGregor was industry minister he heard that West Indians had difficulties setting up their own businesses. So he organized a conference for Afro-Caribbean entrepreneurs, expecting about thirty to turn up. Judge his surprise when he found the meeting packed out with 150. It is a curious thing that, as *Guardian* reporter Leslie Goffe discovered,[3] West Indians from Britain who have gone to the United States are doing well in business. This suggests very strongly that there is no barrier to economic advance within West Indian culture but that there is some psychological factor peculiar to the situation in Britain which is holding them back. The Asian experience would suggest that this factor is not racism. My own view is that Britain's blacks have a huge potential for their own success and for the contribution they can make to national life. The principal reason why they have so far fallen short of fulfilling it is because they have been over-exposed to the combined forces of the race lobby and the left, making excuses in anticipation of their economic failure before they have even begun to try. They have been targeted with the propaganda of those who for their own purposes want Britain's blacks to regard themselves as underdogs and to believe that the 'system', meaning competitive capitalism, is against them. There are indications that the new generation of black British are seeing through all that. They have a future full of promise if they recognize one thing: precisely because it is colour-blind, the free market is their friend.

NOTES

1
A Mania for Our Time

1. *Anti-Racism, an Assault on Education and Value*, ed. Frank Palmer, Sherwood Press, 1986.
2. Ibid.
3. Ibid.
4. A reference to Peter Newsam, Chairman of the Commission for Racial Equality.
5. *Mail on Sunday*, 26 October 1986.
6. *Daily Telegraph*, 3 October 1986.
7. *Daily Mail*, 7 November 1986.
8. *Northern Daily Mail*, 29 October 1986.
9. Ibid., 14 February 1985.
10. Ibid., 13 September 1985.
11. Ibid., 13 December 1986.
12. Ibid., 9 August 1985.
13. *Daily Telegraph*, 6 July 1985.
14. *New Standard*, 21 November 1986.
15. *Daily Mail*, 20 June 1986.
16. Ibid., 5 May 1983.
17. *Daily Mail*, 7 January 1985.
18. Ibid., 1 July 1986.
19. Ibid., 21 May 1986.
20. *Sun*, 19 September 1985.
21. *New Standard*, 20 January 1986.
22. *Northern Daily Mail*, 28 February 1986.
23. *Daily Mail*, 16 October 1985.
24. Ibid., 12 August 1986.
25. Ibid., 30 October 1986.
26. Ibid., 17 March 1986.
27. Ibid., 5 December 1986.
28. Ibid., 2 May 1984.
29. Ibid., 5 May 1984.

30. Ibid., 17 August 1985.
31. Ibid., 1 January 1987.

2

The Emotional Fuels of Anti-Racism

1. *It ain't Half Racist, Mum*, ed. Phil Cohen and Carl Gardner, Comedia Publishing, 1982.
2. *English History 1914–1945*, A.J.P. Taylor, Oxford University Press, 1965.
3. *Why Six Million Died*, Arthur D. Morse, Secker & Warburg, 1968.
4. *Anti-Racism*, op. cit.
5. *The Rise and Fall of the Third Reich*, William L. Shirer, Secker & Warburg, 1960.
6. *Prelude to Genocide*, Simon Taylor, Duckworth, 1985.
7. *Anti-Racism*, op. cit.
8. *History of the Modern World*, Paul Johnson, Weidenfeld & Nicolson, 1983; and, for the Stalin era, *The Great Terror*, Robert Conquest, Macmillan, 1968.
9. *This War Called Peace*, Brian Crozier, Drew Middleton and Jeremy Murray Brown, Sherwood Press, 1984.
10. *Spectator*, 7 February 1987.
11. *The Nation-Killers*, Robert Conquest, Sphere Books, 1972.
12. *The Economics and Politics of Race*, Thomas Sowell, William Morrow & Co., 1982.
13. *Markets and Minorities*, Thomas Sowell, Basil Blackwell, 1981.
14. *Reality and Rhetoric*, P.T. Bauer, Weidenfeld & Nicolson, 1984.
15. *The Irish in Britain*, Kevin O'Connor, Sigwick & Jackson, 1972.
16. *Race and Politics*, Mohammed Anwar, Tavistock Publications, 1986.
17. *Immigration and Race in British Politics*, Paul Foot, Penguin, 1965.
18. *Colour and Citizenship*, the Institute of Race Relations, Oxford University Press, 1969.
19. *Freedom and Reality*, Enoch Powell, Batsford, 1969.

3

Race Discrimination, the Quango Non-Cure

1. *Race and Law*, Anthony Lester and Geoffrey Bindman, Penguin, 1972.
2. *Roy Jenkins*, John Campbell, Weidenfeld & Nicolson, 1983.
3. *The Castle Diaries 1964–70*, Barbara Castle, Weidenfeld & Nicolson, 1984.
4. Hansard, 16 November 1961.
5. *Towards Tomorrow*, Fenner Brockway, Hart-Davis, MacGibbon, 1977.
6. *Daily Telegraph*, 27 October 1969.
7. *The Times*, 25 November 1969 and *Daily Telegraph* 17 December 1969.
8. *Daily Mail*, 21 November 1969.
9. Ibid., 1 November 1969.
10. Ibid., 5 May 1970.
11. *Daily Telegraph*, 13 April 1970.
12. *Daily Mail*, 31 January 1970.

13. *The Times*, 19 February 1970.
14. *Daily Mail*, 20 January 1971.
15. Ibid., 26 March 1971.
16. *The Awkward Warrior*, Geoffrey Goodman, Davis-Poynte, 1979.
17. *Northern Daily Mail*, 4 December 1971.
18. *Daily Telegraph*, 22 March 1975; ibid., 16 June 1976.
19. *Guardian*, 21 January 1971.
20. *Freedom and Reality*, op. cit.

4

The Urge to Affirmative Action

1. *Against Equality*, ed. William Letwin, Macmillan, 1983.
2. 'Against Equality Again', J.R. Lucas, *Against Equality*, op. cit.
3. 'Race and Affirmative Action', John Bowers and Suzanne Franks, Fabian Tract 471, 1980.
4. *Daily Mail*, 24 October 1983.
5. Ibid., 28 August 1978.
6. *Daily Telegraph*, 30 July 1986.
7. *Daily Mail*, 30 July 1982.
8. *The Times*, 18 June 1982.
9. *Sunday Telegraph*, 6 December 1981.
10. *Daily Telegraph*, 5 May 1982.
11. *The Times*, 15 October 1980.
12. 'Immigration Control Procedures', a summary of the CRE report produced by the National Association of Community Relations Councils, 1985.
13. 'Loading the Law', Alan Little and Diana Robins, Commission for Racial Equality, July 1982.
14. 'Employment Prospects for Chinese Youth in Britain', Alfred Chan, Commission for Racial Equality, July 1986.
15. *Daily Telegraph*, 15 August 1982.
16. *Daily Mail*, 6 October 1981.
17. 'Report on the Seminar on Racism Awareness Training', Commission for Racial Equality, October 1984.
18. 'Housing Need Among Ethnic Minorities', Commission for Racial Equality, December 1977.
19. 'Racial Equality and Social Policies in London', Commission for Racial Equality, August 1980.
20. 'Racial Equality and the Youth Training Scheme', Commission for Racial Equality, October 1984.
21. First Report of the Home Affairs Committee, HMSO, 1981.
22. *Daily Telegraph*, 21 September 1976.
23. Ibid., 10 September 1983.
24. *Guardian*, 7 March 1984.
25. CRE Annual Report, 1985; see Appendix 5.

5
Lessons from America

1. The Scarman Report, Lord Scarman, Pelican Books, 1982.
2. *Economic Affairs*, December/January 1986/7.
3. 'The New Black Intellectual', Murray Friedman, *Commentary*, June 1980.
4. *America: A Minority Viewpoint*, Walter E. Williams, Hoover Institute Press, 1982.
5. *Policy Review*, July 1978.
6. See in particular the following three books by Sowell: *Race and Economics*, Longmans, 1975; *Markets and Minorities*, Blackwell, 1981; *The Economics and Politics of Race*, William Morrow & Co., 1983.
7. *Markets and Minorities*, op. cit.
8. *Losing Ground*, Charles Murray, Basic Books, 1984.
9. *The Triumph of Politics*, David Stockman, the Bodley Head, 1986.
10. 'A Conservative Vision of Welfare', Stuart M. Butler, *Policy Review*, Spring 1987.
11. 'Who Speaks for American Blacks', Glenn C. Lowry, *Commentary*, January 1986.

6
Race and Riot

1. CRE Annual Report, 1985.
2. *Daily Telegraph*, 28 July 1981.
3. Scarman Report, op. cit.
4. *Daily Mail*, 13 April 1981.
5. Ibid, 11 July 1981.
6. *Daily Telegraph*, 28 July 1981.
7. *Commentary*, September 1977.
8. *Economist*, 18 July 1981.
9. *Daily Mail*, 13 July 1981.
10. *Sunday Telegraph*, 27 May 1984.
11. *The Times*, 10 September 1984.
12. Ibid., 25 July 1986.
13. *Guardian*, 20 October 1984.
14. *Daily Telegraph*, 30 October 1984.
15. *Daily Express*, 8 October 1985.
16. *Daily Mail*, 28 July 1982.
17. *Mail on Sunday*, 10 June 1984.
18. *Daily Telegraph*, 18 October 1985.
19. *Are the Police Fair?*, David Waddington, Social Affairs Unit, 1983.
20. *Daily Mail*, 8 October 1985.
21. *Daily Telegraph*, 9 October 1985.
22. *Independent*, 10 January 1987.
23. *The Sunday Times*, 3 May 1987.
24. *Daily Mail*, 11 September 1985.

25. Ibid., 28 February 1986.
26. Ibid., 21 February 1986.
27. Ibid., 15 September 1985.
28. Ibid., 21 January 1986.

7
Inner City Innocence

1. *Faith in the City*, Church House Publishing, 1985.
2. *Daily Mail*, 2 December 1985.
3. Ibid.
4. *Faith in the City*, op. cit.
5. *Colonial Immigrants in a British City*, J. Rex and S. Tomlinson, Routledge & Keegan Paul, 1979.
6. *Reversing Racism*, Social Affairs Unit, 1984.
7. *Independent*, 8 January 1987.
8. *Asian Housing in Britain*, J.G. Davies, Social Affairs Unit, 1985.
9. *Daily Mail*, 12 June 1981.
10. *Daily Telegraph*, 15 March 1985.
11. *Economist*, 18 July 1981.
12. *Good Council Guide*, Paul Beresford, Centre for Policy Studies, 1987.
13. *Space on Earth*, Charles Knevitt, Thames Methuen, 1985.
14. Scarman Report, op. cit.
15. 'Why There is No Such Thing as a One-Parent Family', Patricia Morgan, *Daily Telegraph*, 6 July 1983.
16. J. Cheetham, S. Ahmed, J. Small (eds.), *Social Work with Black Children and Their Families*, Batsford, 1986.
17. Quoted in *Denying Homes to Black Children*, David Dale, Social Affairs Unit, 1987.
18. Ibid.
19. 'The Deserving Poor', *Economist*, 25 April 1987.

8
The False Promise of Politics

1. *Race and Politics*, op. cit.
2. *The Greek View of Life*, G. Lowes Dickinson, Methuen, 1949.
3. 'America's Apartheid', *National Review*, 8 May 1987.
4. *The Racial Politics of Militant in Liverpool*, Runnymede Trust, 1986.
5. Ibid.
6. 'Black People and Politics in Britain', Marian Fitzgerald, Runnymede Trust, 1987.
7. Ibid.
8. *The Times*, 15 October 1985.
9. *Guardian*, 18 February 1987.
10. 'Black People and Politics', op. cit.
11. *Sunday Telegraph*, 15 December 1985.

12. *Daily Mail*, 16 July 1985.
13. *The Times*, 2 October 1986.
14. *Independent*, 7 March 1987.
15. *Sunday Telegraph*, 15 March 1987.
16. *Daily Mail*, 10 April 1987.
17. *Daily Mail*, 13 April 1987.

9
Anti-Racism versus Freedom

1. *Parasitism and Subversion: the South American Case*, Stanislav Andreski, Weidenfeld & Nicolson, 1966.
2. CRE Annual Report, 1985.
3. 'Contract Compliance for the UK', John Carr, Fabian Society, January 1987.
4. *America: A Minority Viewpoint*, Walter Williams, Hoover Institution, November 1982.
5. *Daily Mail*, 27 October 1983.
6. Ibid., 12 April 1986.
7. 'The Wayward Curriculum', ed. Dennis O'Keefe, Social Affairs Unit, 1986.
8. 'Television in a Multi-racial Society', Muhammad Anwar and Anthony Shang, Commission for Racial Equality, 1984.
9. *Daily Telegraph*, 5 October 1985.
10. *Week End*, 18 January 1984.
11. *The Times*, 30 May 1978.
12. *Daily Express*, 27 September 1985.

10
Race Harmony in a Free Society

1. The *Sunday Times*, 26 February 1984.
2. *Daily Mail*, 31 December 1982.
3. *Guardian*, 11 June 1986.

APPENDIX

The Race Relations Act 1976: Survey of Main Proposals for Change

Discrimination and the Scope of the Act

1 (i) Either by direct statement or by use of illustration as to what is meant by 'on racial grounds', the Act (without the need for reference to case-law) should make the position clear that *direct discrimination* does not necessarily involve a racial motive.

(ii) A new definition of *indirect discrimination* is required making unlawful any practice, policy or situation which is continued, allowed, or introduced and which has a *significant adverse impact* on a particular racial group and which cannot be *demonstrated to be necessary*.

(iii) The legislation should exemplify the meaning of *significant adverse impact*, for example by an illustration in which a 20 per cent difference in impact between racial groups is treated as significant.

(iv) The legislation should exemplify the test of what is *necessary* with illustrative formulations for each of the various fields in which the Act applies. For example, in a matter involving employment it will need to be shown that what is having the adverse impact is necessary to ensure that the functions of the job are carried out safely and competently and that the same end cannot be achieved in a less discriminatory manner.

2 Protection against victimisation for invoking the Act is at present incomplete. The remedy for victimisation should be redefined so that there is protection against a person's suffering any detriment whatever as a result of his or her doing any of the acts listed in section 2 1(a)–(d) (involvement in allegations, proceedings, etc. under the Act).

3 At present the Act covers discrimination on the grounds of colour, race, nationality or ethnic or national origins. The question whether religious discrimination should be made unlawful and, if so, in what circumstances, needs to be considered in a wider context than that of an amendment to the Race Relations Act.

Exemptions from the Act

4 At present a wide range of actions, governmental in nature, are outside the ambit of the Act. The definition relating to the provision of 'goods, facilities and services' in the Act should make it clear that it extends to all areas of governmental and regulatory activity whether central or local such as acts in the course of immigration control, the prison and police services, and planning control.

5 The Race Relations Act is by its own terms subordinated to a wide range of rules existing or future with which it conflicts. The basic legislation making discrimination unlawful should be superior to earlier Acts and all subordinate legislation or other forms of rule-making. Where Government requires as a matter of policy that discrimination should be permitted on grounds of birth, nationality, descent or residence, this should be provided for expressly by statute.

6 Work experience trainees are not regarded as 'employed' and therefore not covered by the main provisions of the Act. They should be brought directly within the protection of the Act as though they were employees and not continue to rely on the more limited and little known protection given by designation under section 13.

7 The present exemption for seamen recruited abroad in section 9 of the Act should be repealed by use of the special power provided for that purpose in section 73 of the Act. Section 8 of the Act should be amended so that the Act applies to employment on board a ship registered at a port of registry in Great Britain wherever the work takes place and not as at present if the work is wholly outside Great Britain. Corresponding provision should be made for employment on aircraft and hovercraft.

Proving Discrimination and Ajudication

8 The burden of proof in direct discrimination cases should build on the established case-law and be set out in the statute. The person against whom discrimination is alleged, in circumstances consistent with less favourable treatment on racial grounds, should be required to establish non-racial grounds for that treatment since he or she is the person best able to show the grounds for his or her own actions.

9 Where a respondent deliberately and without reasonable excuse either omits a reply, or gives an evasive or equivocal reply, to a questionnaire pursuant to section 65 of the Act, there should be a duty, rather than a discretion, on the part of the tribunal of fact to draw the inference that it considers just.

10 A discrimination division within the industrial tribunal system should be established to hear both employment and non-employment race and sex discrimination cases. The County Court jurisdiction for non-employment cases should go. The discrimination division should be able to call upon the services of High Court Judges for more complex cases and should have full remedial powers. Personnel of the division should be available to hear other types of industrial tribunal cases when not sitting in the division.

11 In accordance with the recommendations of the Royal Commission on Legal Services, legal aid should be extended to cover racial discrimination cases in tribunals.

Formal Investigations and Law Enforcement

12 Subsection 49(4) of the Act should be repealed. This would mean that the effect of the *Prestige* case would be reversed and the Commission's powers 'to conduct a formal investigation for any purpose connected with the carrying out of' its duties (s.48) would thereby be clearly established.

13 The Commission's non-discrimination notices, issued as a consequence of formal investigations, are subject to appeal. In their place, the Commission should have the power to take evidence of discrimination directly to an independent tribunal of fact seeking a finding that discrimination has occurred and appropriate remedies. This access to the tribunal should not be conditional upon a formal investigation having taken place, though in practice this would often be the case.

14 A non-discrimination notice is a remedy in the hands of the Commission but such a notice cannot prescribe particular changes in practice. If the remedy was instead placed in the hands of an independent tribunal, the tribunal should be able to order particular changes in practice.

Remedies

15 (i) The remedy referred to in Proposal 14 should be a remedy generally available to the independent tribunal of fact to deal with potential future discrimination. The tribunal of fact should be under a duty to consider whether such a remedy is appropriate in any case where discrimination is proved.

(ii) The Commission should have the power to join in any proceedings in which discrimination is alleged to draw the attention of the tribunal of fact to the potential for future discrimination in the situation.

(iii) In any case brought by the Commission – see Proposal 13 – the tribunal of fact should have the power to award compensation to any person it finds to have suffered unlawful discrimination either named or otherwise sufficiently identified provided that any such person joins the proceedings within a specified time and seeks the compensation.

16 Non-monetary remedies. In addition to the remedies now available a full range of mandatory orders should be available to the tribunal of fact.

(i) A preventive remedy should be available where a person has stated a directly discriminatory intention to avoid that intention being put into practice.

(ii) The tribunal of fact should have the power, in appropriate cases where discrimination is proved, to order those positive action measures such as special training or encouragement of members of particular racial groups which are at present permitted as voluntary measures in the circumstances set out in the Act.

(iii) The remedy referred to in Proposals 14 and 15(i) should apply also to the whole area of education. Instead of the Secretary of State having powers under section 19(2) and (3) of the Act, the tribunal of fact should have the power to order changes in practice to deal with potential future discrimination.

(iv) In employment cases interim relief should be available to preserve a complainant's position pending a hearing provided that the relief is sought promptly and the remedy appears appropriate to the tribunal of fact.

(v) In employment cases it should be possible for the tribunal of fact to order appointment, promotion, reinstatement or reengagement where it appears appropriate to do so.

17 Monetary remedies. The provision of compensation should be improved as follows:

(a) There should be a prescribed norm figure by way of compensation for injury to feelings.

(b) Compensation should be payable where indirect discrimination is proved and the present exception in s.57(3) removed.

(c) The tribunal of fact should be able to award continuing payments of compensation until a stipulated event such as promotion or engagement occurs.

(d) The statutory limit to compensation in employment cases set out in section 56(2) of the Act should be removed.

18 The special defence provided under section 32(3) of the Act should be removed. It covers the case where an employer can show that he or she took 'such steps as were reasonably practicable to prevent the employee from doing that act, or from doing in the course of his employment acts of that description'.

Mechanisms for Bringing about Change

19 The Commission's code-making power under section 47 should not be restricted to the field of employment, but should be extended to include other areas.

20 The Secretary of State should be given powers to prescribe ethnic record-keeping of (i) employees in different grades and applicants for employment and (ii) recipients of housing or other service provision by public bodies. The orders prescribing the keeping of records should be capable of limitation by (i) area of the country (ii) types of activity (iii) duration of the record-keeping. There should be a power in the Commission to require returns to be made where record-keeping has been prescribed. Safeguards against abuse of the information should be enacted.

21 Where there is agreement between the Commission and a body on specific practices to be adopted, the Commission should have the power to accept legally-binding and enforceable undertakings by that body to adopt those practices. The undertakings should be recorded in a public register.

22(i) The general statutory duty imposed on local authorities by section 71 of the Act should be amended to conform to those imposed on the Commission by section 43(1)(a) and (b) with regard to each of the various functions of the authorities. Those duties are 'to work towards the elimination of discrimination and to promote equality of opportunity and good relations between persons of different racial groups generally'.

(ii) This duty should be extended to all bodies carrying on a service or undertaking of a public nature (for a definition see section 75(5) of the Act).

(iii) Public bodies as above should be required by law to publish, in their annual reports or separately, annual programmes and reports to enable the public to evaluate their work in the field of race.

23(i) An employer should be permitted to give special training to persons of particular racial groups, whether or not they are his or her employees, where there is under-representation in the workforce as defined in section 38; and section 38 should be widened accordingly so that the training aspect of the provision covers non-employees. An employer would then not need to rely upon designation under section 37. Training schemes for young people such as apprenticeships should be explicitly covered by such a provision.

(ii) An employer should be entitled where there is under-representation of a particular racial group in the workforce (as defined in section 38) to carry out a policy of preferring a member of that group for employment in the narrowly confined situation where competing applicants for employment are equally well qualified to carry out the job in question.

Extract from *Review of the Race Relations Act 1976: Proposals for Change*, CRE, July 1985.

167

INDEX

169